文人树盆景

LITERATI STYLE PENJING

LITERATI STYLE PENJING

Chinese Bonsai Masterworks

By ZHAO QINGQUAN
Translated by LIU HAIMING

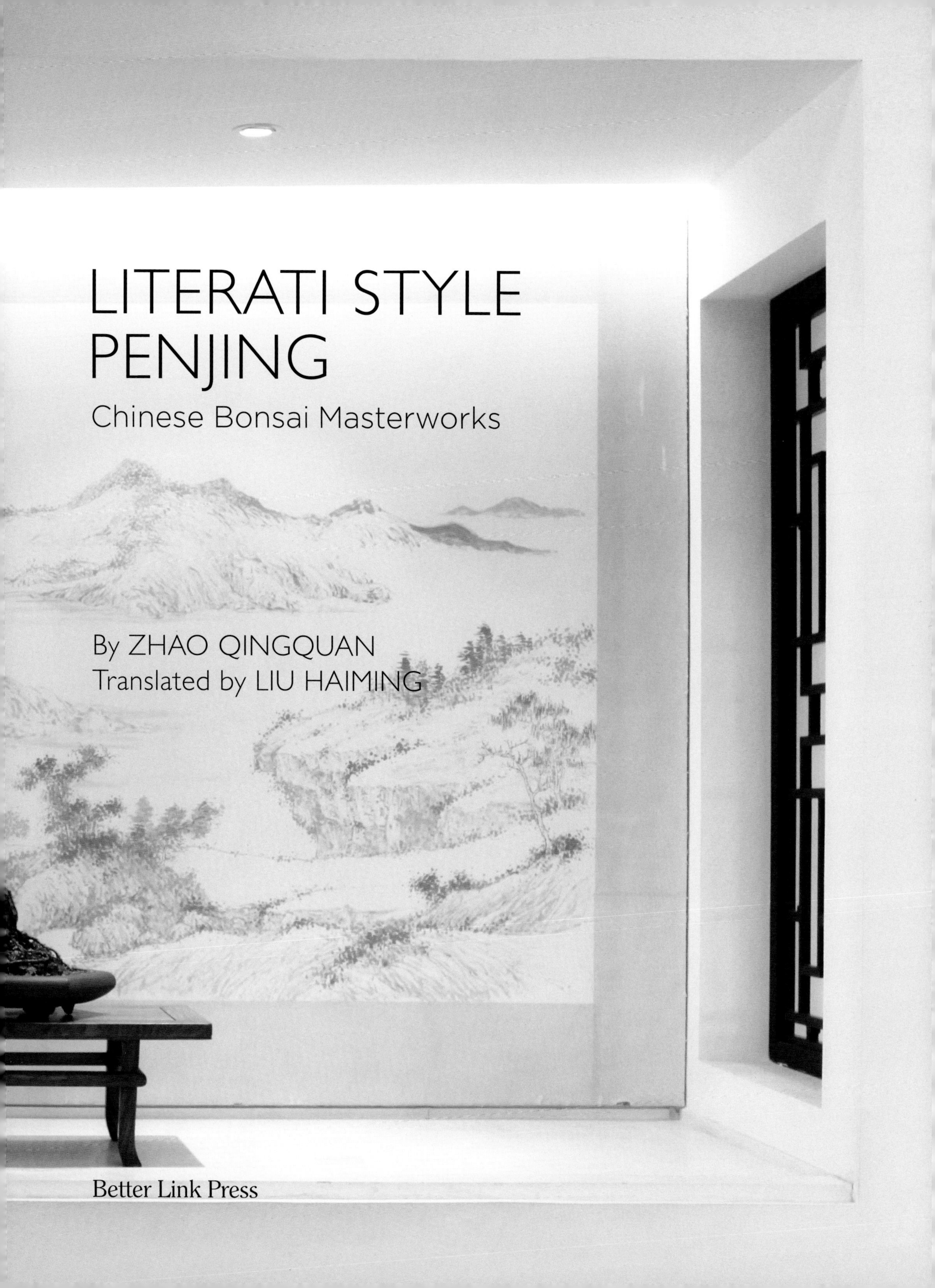

Better Link Press

Text by Zhao Qingquan
Photographs by Zhao Qingquan, Han Xuenian, Wu Chengfa, Zheng Zhilin, Xu Hao, Zheng Yongtai, Zhao Yi, Shen Songsong, Chen Chang, Sun Jianjun
Foreword by Thomas S. Elias
Translation by Liu Haiming
Cover Design by Wang Wei
Interior Design by Li Jing, Hu Bin (Yuan Yinchang Design Studio)

Editors: Yang Xiaohe, Wu Yuezhou, Kirstin Mattson
Editorial Director: Zhang Yicong

ISBN: 978-1-60220-018-0

Address any comments about *Literati Style Penjing: Chinese Bonsai Masterworks* to:

Better Link Press
99 Park Ave
New York, NY 10016
USA

or

Shanghai Press and Publishing Development Co., Ltd.
Floor 5, No. 390 Fuzhou Road, Shanghai, China (200001)
Email: sppd@sppdbook.com

Printed in China by Shanghai Donnelley Printing Co., Ltd.

3 5 7 9 10 8 6 4

On page 1
Fig. 1 *Vicissitudes of Life*
Species: Hedge sageretia (*Sageretia theezans*)
Height: 60 cm
Age: Approx. 50 years
Designer: Zhao Qingquan
Introduction: The trunk displays a curvy "S" shape, with bark showing great aged character. While an old specimen, it exhibits vigor and verdant small leaves.

On pages 2–3
Fig. 2 For display in exhibition, place literati penjing in well-lit and ventilated space, with perhaps a Chinese landscape painting as backdrop

Right
Fig. 3 *Flowing Grace*
Species: Chinese red pine (*Pinus massoniana*)
Spread: 140 cm
Age: Approx. 50 years
Designer: Han Xuenian
Introduction: A cliff-hanging style pine, with the trunk curving downward in a cascading line like water falling over a cliff, it epitomizes vigor and a flowing grace.

CONTENTS

Fig. 4 *Drunken Stupor*
Species: Hedge sageretia (*Sageretia theezans*)
Height: 110 cm
Age: 50 years
Designer: Wu Chengfa
Introduction: The trunk curves in a bold sweep to the upper left, with the left primary branch extending in a dramatic cascade, conveying a sense of freedom and abandon. The exposed roots spread out, anchoring the tree.

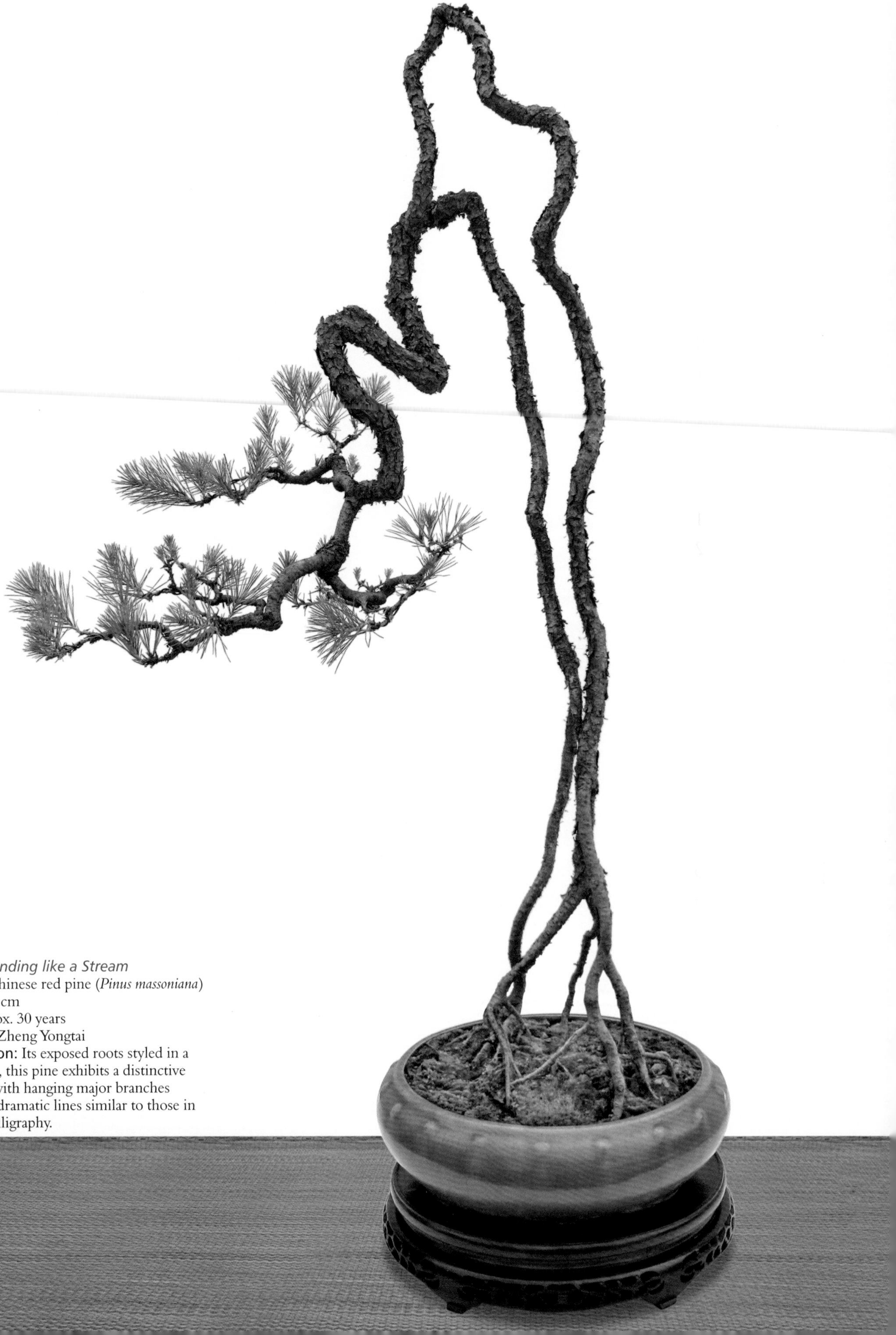

Fig. 5 *Winding like a Stream*
Species: Chinese red pine (*Pinus massoniana*)
Height: 95 cm
Age: Approx. 30 years
Designer: Zheng Yongtai
Introduction: Its exposed roots styled in a trunk form, this pine exhibits a distinctive character, with hanging major branches producing dramatic lines similar to those in Chinese calligraphy.

CONTENTS

Fig. 6 *Lofty and Unyielding Character*
Species: Taiwan juniper (*Juniperus formosana*)
Height: 120 cm
Age: 80 years
Designer: Wu Chengfa
Introduction: With its long bare trunk and sparse branches and leaves, this penjing aims to portray the character of the Chinese literati and their preference for a simple, rustic life.

序言 | FOREWORD

The literati style is the most challenging and the most rewarding form to create, if done correctly, of all the different styles of penjing. Taking a narrow trunked tree and shaping it to give an expression of aloofness is difficult. A thin trunk, just a few branches, and relatively few leaves are primary characteristics of the literati style. These features help to convey the feelings of remoteness and aloofness just as a pine struggles to survive in a crevice high in the Huangshan.

The feelings a literati penjing conveys are often identified with the reclusive nature of scholars. Many people in western countries have difficulty understanding and appreciating the literati style, unless they have studied aspects of Asian aesthetics. Looking to nature and the struggle of trees to survive in severe conditions in high mountain rocky places led to the understanding and development of this style.

Few artists can master this technique to make an excellent literati penjing and fewer still have the ability and background to properly instruct others on all aspects of this style. This challenge has been met by penjing master Zhao Qingquan in this book.

This volume is the finest work on the literati style ever produced in any language. For the first time, Zhao provides us with the aesthetic and cultural backgrounds needed to understand and appreciate the beautiful aloofness of the literati penjing. His ability to provide clear, well-illustrated information about basic techniques is typical of this accomplished teacher, artist and friend to the world's penjing and bonsai communities.

I have known Zhao Qingquan for many years, admired his artistic skills, and studied his English language penjing books. He combines the extraordinary skills of a leading artist with the amazing ability to effectively communicate and educate people, regardless of their nationality. Now we have his newest and, perhaps, his most important contribution, *Literati Style Penjing*. I congratulate Zhao Qingquan on this significant accomplishment and I predict that this work will be a classic reference for generations to come.

Thomas Elias
President
Bonsai Clubs International

Fig. 8 *Dancer*
Species: Five-needle pine (*Pinus parviflora*)
Height: 65 cm
Age: 38 years
Designer: Zhao Qingquan
Introduction: The natural shape of this literati penjing evokes the unaffected elegance and ease of a masterful dancer.

Facing page
Fig. 7 *Brilliance in Autumn*
Species: Firethorn (*Pyracantha fortuneana*)
Height: 65 cm
Age: 30 years
Designer: Zhao Qingquan
Introduction: The Chinese firethorn produces delightful small white flowers in spring and summer, and in the fall produces bright-colored small berries, which turn intense red and stay on the plant until early spring, promising joy and luck. With a curvy trunk and sparse but well-spaced foliage, this firethorn has a distinct literati feel.

前言 PREFACE

An important traditional art in China, penjing, meaning "tray scenery," aims at "seeing the large from the tiny." Working with plants, rocks, soil and water, penjing artists seek to evoke magnificent natural scenery through miniature representations, employing artistic vision and skillful plant cultivation techniques in creating their compositions. Penjing often serves as a method of self-expression, conveying personal emotions.

Also known as *penzai* (read in Japanese as "bonsai"), the art form originated in China, and was later brought to Japan in the Southern Song Dynasty of China (1127–1279), roughly corresponding to the late Heian period in Japan (794–1192). It has remained popular for centuries, and has grown to reach a worldwide audience since its introduction to the West from Japan in modern times.

Penjing in the literati style are in a category of their own. This particular style of penjing relates to the aspirations of the elite scholar-bureaucrats of imperial China. They had a refined and elegant sensibility in their approach to many art forms, including poetry and painting. Therefore literati style penjing usually feature elongated trunks with few branches, and idiosyncratic lines imbued with stark simplicity and grace. Though Eastern in sensibility, penjing has caught on in the West in recent years.

The style can only be loosely defined, being difficult to describe in precise terms. It is inherently related to the literati class and literati painting in China, not merely adopting the name but also the upright character, refinement, aspirations and stylistic preferences. Literati penjing share the same spirit and approach to artistic expression inherent in literati paintings, affirming a yearning to escape to a freer style.

In imperial China, the strict system of civil service examinations gave rise to a class of scholars who studied to become civil servants. This convergence of officialdom and learning produced a unique social class of scholar-bureaucrats, most of whom were well educated and versed in art. They were a mainstay of society, profoundly influencing Chinese culture in the age of antiquity, and bringing forth a distinctive style of art—the literati painting.

The art of Chinese penjing, from its very beginning, was a pursuit of the scholarly class. Literati style penjing represents a consummate level in this pursuit. It is difficult now to pin down when the style first appeared, though it is without doubt rooted in the cultural movement of literati art and, at a more profound level, the three major philosophical traditions of ancient China: Confucianism, Taoism and *Chan* (or Zen) Buddhism.

Literati style trees display rugged, vigorous forms, with obvious visual characteristics that are often featured in traditional Chinese landscape paintings. They are not necessarily representative of typical tree forms in nature. Rather than mere natural representations, they are seen more as a statement of artistic aspiration. The works strive to approximate *huajing*, *shijing* and *chanjing*, meaning respectively, "flavor of (ink) painting," "poetic state" and "the realm of Zen."

Therefore a literati style penjing may appear simple, yet it is most expressive with layers of subtle meaning. Achieving a truly masterful piece can be difficult, not because of technical challenges but rather aesthetic considerations. Literati penjing is unique in the world of Chinese penjing, and is most adept at expressing the artist's character, refinement, innate qualities and

Facing page
Fig. 9 *A Distant Gaze*
Species: Japanese black pine (*Pinus thunbergii*)
Height: 105 cm
Age: 30 years
Designer: Zhao Qingquan
Introduction: Inspired by a painting of Ma Yuan, this penjing aims to capture a sense of artlessness, simplicity, aloofness and serenity. Its slanting trunks, joined at the roots, and sparse but rugged branches create an elegant structure.

Facing page
Fig. 10 *A Sharp Sense of Integrity*
Species: Taiwan juniper (*Juniperus formosana*)
Height: 115 cm
Age: Over 90 years
Designer: Zhao Qingquan
Introduction: This specimen shows a towering trunk with a clear structure. The first primary branch twists and is bent downward along the trunk, and this twisting branch echoes and compliments the straight trunk. The grey deadwood of the upright trunk, the *sheli* or *shari*, contrasts with the dark brown living veins, evoking a sharp sense of integrity.

Fig. 11 *When Willows Were Fresh and Green*
Species: Chinese weeping cypress (*Cupressus funebris endl*)
Height: 105 cm
Age: Approx. 30 years
Designer: Zhao Qingquan
Introduction: The drooping branches of the weeping cypress were styled to demonstrate characteristics of the graceful weeping willow. The specimen has a slightly curvy trunk with upturned primary branches and drooping secondary branches, forming delicate, smooth and rounded lines. This penjing calls to mind two famous lines from a classic Chinese poem, "At first, when we set out / the willows were fresh and green," evoking nostalgia for the bygone.

emotional depth.

I have a special passion for literati penjing, having been much devoted to their creation and study over many years. This book, based on my learning and experience, covers the concept, aesthetics, cultural origins, techniques, and care and maintenance of literati penjing, richly illustrated by examples of literati trees that I have created. This book is for penjing enthusiasts, as an informative and practical guide, as well as for others interested in Chinese culture in general. It is my hope that this pleasing art of refined elegance will continue to grow in popularity and appreciation.

My thanks go to Dr. Thomas S. Elias, President of Bonsai Clubs International, for the foreword he wrote, and to the other penjing masters who provided photographs for this book.

审美 CHAPTER ONE Aesthetics

All fine penjing specimens are joint creations of the artist and nature. They feature a highly appealing blend of nature and art, a characteristic for which penjing is appreciated. Chinese penjing generally fall into one of the three categories classified by their source material, subject matter and design: tree penjing, landscape penjing or water-and-land penjing.

Tree penjing present images of natural trees and plants, in pots, using woody plants as primary source materials. Landscape penjing, on the other hand, feature island and mountain landscapes with carefully chosen rocks. Water-and-land penjing are a hybrid of the first two types, depicting not only a landscape consisting of mountains and water, but also images of trees and plants, employing materials that may include plants, rocks, soil and water. Literati penjing is an approach or style within the tree penjing category.

The artistic beauty of penjing lies in naturalness, design and imagery. Literati penjing share many of the aesthetic attributes of other types of penjing, while giving special emphasis to the line and space created by the tree, which can help convey the character, mood and aspirations typically associated with a literati, or "man of culture." They also attempt to approximate an artistic and poetic state, and invoke the realm of *Chan* Buddhism (known as Zen in Japanese transliteration).

Fig. 12 *Wind in the Maple*
Species: Japanese maple (*Acer palmatum*)
Height: 80 cm (main tree)
Age: 25 years
Designer: Zhao Qingquan
Introduction: This literati penjing of the forest group style features a group of Japanese maples. The main tree is the largest and tallest, complimented by other trees forming a gorgeous forest, producing pale yellow new leaves and tiny purple flowers in the spring.

Fig. 13 *Father and Son*
Species: Chinese hackberry (*Celtis sinensis*)
Height: 115 cm
Age: 50 years
Designer: Wu Chengfa
Introduction: The contrasts between the primary and secondary, and sparseness and denseness, are evident in this twin-trunk composition. The light green hue of the trunk gives it a distinct character.

Fig. 14 Consistency in line, with trunk slanting to the left and exposed roots extending right, is visually pleasing.

Fig. 15 The lean trunk of this pine is scaly with a weathered look.

Fig. 16 Deadwood (*sheli*) accompanied by twisting living veins and verdant leaves offers a striking contrast between living and withered.

1. Naturalness

The primary materials used in penjing works come from nature. Much of the naturalness of penjing results from the artistic rearrangements of living materials—trees and plants, grass and lichen—that change with the seasons and over time.

Naturalness is essential to the appealing beauty of penjing. The same applies to the category of literati penjing. Such naturalness is reflected in the design of a specimen's roots, trunk, foliage, flowers or fruits; its structure and shape; and its morphing with the seasons.

Roots. The shape and placement of tree roots vary enormously by species and growing conditions. Some have roots that fan out broadly or are highly exposed while others have root systems that are tightly entwined or grow deeply into crevices of rocks. All can be visually pleasing. Literati trees, however, do not usually have roots that are evenly spread out or highly exposed. Their roots tend to have a steadfast quality that matches the shape of the trunk (fig. 14).

Trunks. A literati tree usually has a slender trunk, which must have an appearance of age. The trunk, securely anchored, should not look overly thick near the base, displaying heaviness. Trunks can vary considerably from tree to tree in shape. While an upright trunk can be towering and majestic, curvy ones demonstrate vigor and gracefulness. Different species show variations in bark texture and color. For example, while the bark of a pine can be thick and scaly (fig. 15), that of junipers has a smooth and shiny look. The bark of diamond-leaf persimmons is strikingly grey, like that of trees depicted in ink and brush paintings. Other colors include dark green (fig. 13), black, grayish brown, red, yellowish brown or purple black. Some tree trunks are half-dead, creating stunning contrasts between deadwood (called *sheli* in Chinese penjing, *shari* in Japanese bonsai) and living veins and foliage, evoking a sense of age and battle against the elements (fig. 16).

Branches. Literati penjing tend to have sparse foliage, with stark lines in the tree form creating strong visual impact. Branches differ in appearance by tree species and through design. Some trees have large and sparse branches while others produce foliage with tiny but dense twigs. Some branches are like deer antlers while others resemble crab legs (figs. 17, 19). Some are straight and strong. Others may be curvy, displaying a sense of rhythm (fig. 18).

Fig. 17 Such spiky twigs of a literati penjing are often described as "elk antlers" (up-turning) or "crab legs" (down-turning).

Fig. 18 *An Old Man in Spring*
Species: Pitanga (*Eugenia uniflora*)
Height: 180 cm
Age: 40 years
Designer: Wu Chengfa
Introduction: The pitanga, with its trunk and branches showing movement, variation and rhythm, demonstrates a fine balance between sparseness and denseness, and a sense of ethereal beauty.

Fig. 19 *Before the Advent of Spring*
Species: Pomegranate (*Punica granatum*)
Height: 80 cm
Age: 25 years
Designer: Xu Hao
Introduction: The "antler" twigs evoke stark autumnal beauty and a poetic yearning for the coming of spring.

Fig. 20 *Flowing Grace*
Species: Japanese maple (*Acer palmatum*)
Height: 45 cm
Age: 10 years
Designer: Zhao Qingquan
Introduction: The simple composition featuring two flowing curves displays a liberal elegance often seen in running style calligraphy. The intense red of the palm-shaped leaves offers a striking sight.

Fig. 21 Flowering plants are cultivated not merely for pleasant appearance but for their symbolism. Virtue and resilience were seen by the literati as characteristics of the winter sweet.

Fig. 22 Diamond-leaf persimmon lit up by the bright yellow offerings of autumn

Leaves. Pines and junipers are preferred for literati penjing, while some deciduous species with small leaves are also used. The leaves of plants have much variations in shape: needle or scale shapes, ovate-oblong to cuneate-obovate, or fan shapes. They can be thick or thin, and tender or tough in feel, with great variations in color too, from light or medium green to deeper greens. Some, being part of flowers, are floral leaves, but others may be green with red edges (fig. 20).

Flowers. Literati penjing are not cultivated for their flowering display, with a few exceptions. Depending on the variety, flowers can vary greatly in shape as well as color (fig. 21).

Fruits. Only a few fruiting plants are used for literati penjing, mostly chosen for their tiny and sparse fruits. They come in a variety of shapes and colors, evocative of emotions and meanings, as fruition signifies the unending cycle of life (fig. 22).

Fig. 23 *Calm Composure*
Species: Sargent's juniper (*Juniperus chinensis var. sargentii*)
Height: 62 cm
Age: 25 years
Designer: Zhao Qingquan
Introduction: This specimen shows elegant naturalness with its trunk twisting upward. Its sparse upper limbs and foliage suggest simplicity and inner calm.

Fig. 24 *Lone Crane*
Species. Airy shaw (*Poilaniella fragilis*)
Height: 125 cm
Age: 80 years
Designer: Wu Chengfa
Introduction: The aged trunk, with a serpentine drooping branch, evokes a sense of proud loneliness.

Fig. 25 *Effortless Contentment*
Species: Japanese black pine (*Pinus thunbergii*)
Height: 60 cm
Age: 40 years
Designer: Chen Chang
Introduction: As the pine ages, it displays a weather-beaten trunk with its drooping primary branch, as if having endured battering by the elements.

Ruggedness. Literati penjing are deemed a rarity among tree penjing. They show striking resemblance to trees grown in a tough environment in the wild. Appearing to have weathered the elements, often in harsh habitats, they exhibit spare foliage, much of it toward the apex or clinging to a few major branches. Literati penjing emulate trees of hardy character (fig. 23), portraying solitude, calm and resilience (fig. 24). They assume increasing agedness as they grow (fig. 25).

Seasonality. Like other styles of penjing, literati trees change color and allure with the seasons. This is especially true with deciduous plants; their pale leaves in spring turn a deep green in summer and russet in the fall. The limbs, bare of leaves, are striking in winter. The seasonal beauty of literati trees, enhanced by hints of humanistic ideals, is one of the reasons why they can be both attractive and inspiring (fig. 26).

Fig. 26 *Leaves Thinning in Cold Wind*
Species: Japanese maple (*Acer palmatum*)
Height: 95 cm
Age: 25 years old
Designer: Xu Hao
Introduction: Japanese maple is a popular penjing species for its dramatic foliage, changing color as the season progresses and thinning in late autumn, evoking feelings for cycles of nature and human life.

2. Line

Traditional Chinese painters, like calligraphers, seal carvers and gardeners, often rely on the use of line in composition—the hallmark of classical Chinese ink and brush painting. Such use of linear aesthetics serves as a device of self-expression.

Literati penjing works feature lean trunks, sparing limbs and foliage, in bold forms heightened by striking lines (fig. 27). An understanding of the arts of classical Chinese calligraphy, seal carving and painting can help enhance appreciation of the linear elements in literati penjing design.

The practice of calligraphy and seal carving was deemed high art in ancient China. The brushstrokes that make up each character form intricate skeins of line, giving expression to personal style. The running style (*caoshu* in Chinese) of seemingly effortless and unrestrained brushwork gives the calligrapher freedom in rendering emotions and inner force (fig. 28). Seal carvings by the renowned

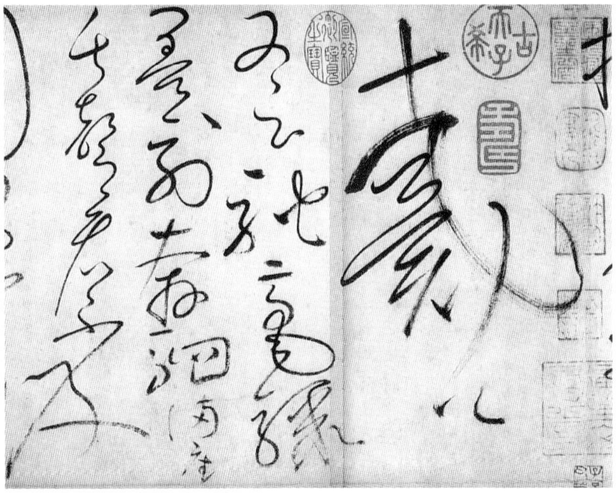

Fig. 28 Detail, calligraphy entitled *Autobiography* by Huai Su (c. 730s–790s), Tang Dynasty (618–907), collection of Palace Museum, Taipei. The brushstrokes are rounded and dashing, almost as if they were steel wires curled and bent, hence the description "steel strokes and silver hooks." The brushwork skirts up, down, left and right as it speeds across the paper, showing a musical rhythm with breathtaking crescendos much like a symphony.

Fig. 27 *Enchanting Grace*
Species: Chinese red pine (*Pinus massoniana*)
Height: 130 cm
Age: Approx. 40 years
Designer: Han Xuenian
Introduction: The source tree was collected from the wild. The design shows a great sense of freedom, violating conventions and highlighting natural vigor.

Fig. 29 Detail, *Eighty-Seven Immortals* by Wu Daozi, Tang Dynasty (618–907), collection of Xu Beihong Memorial Museum

mid-20th century painter Qi Baishi, for example, display bold lines and decisive finish. Like calligraphy and seal carving, the art of literati penjing, with its pronounced linear themes, serves as a medium of self-expression.

Traditional ink and brush painting can trace its lineage to calligraphy, with a similar emphasis on line. Gu Kaizhi (c.345–409), a painter in the Eastern Jin Dynasty (317–420), is said to have first adopted the use of line, which was perfected by later painters. Wu Daozi of the Tang Dynasty (618–907), for example, created portraits with intricate lines depicting robes ruffled by wind (fig. 29). Ma Yuan of the Southern Song Dynasty painted pines with rugged trunks and "spiky branches strong as iron." Zheng Banqiao (1693–1765), an eccentric painter living in the Qing Dynasty (1644–1911), created his iconic images of bamboos and orchids with bold and sparing lines (fig. 30).

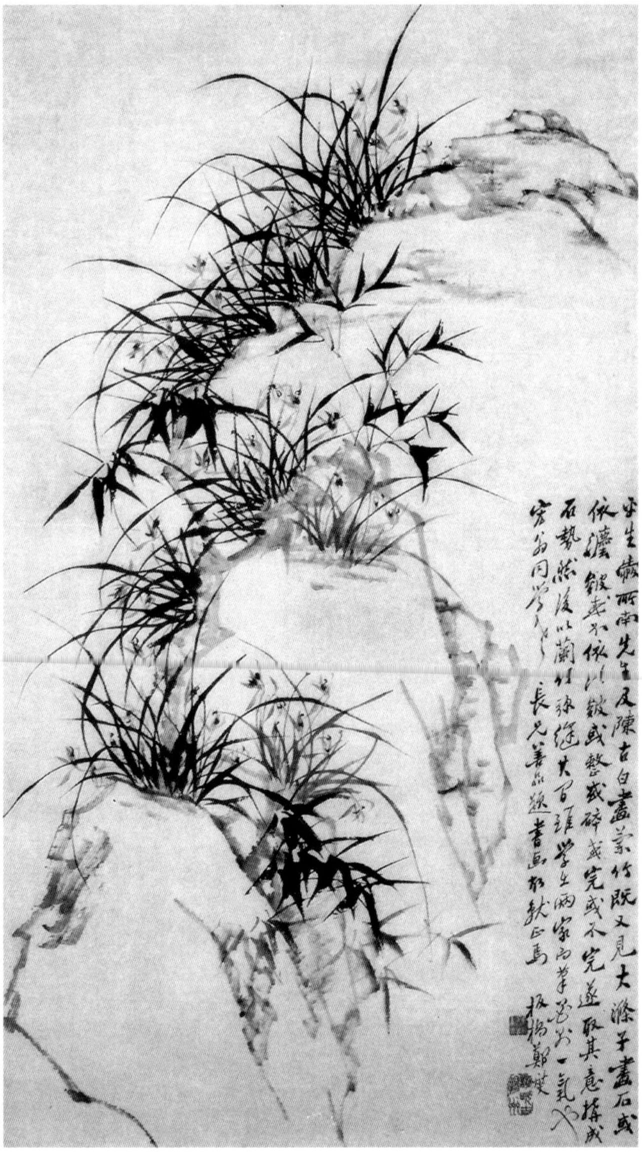

Fig. 30 *Orchids, Bamboo and Rocks* by Zheng Banqiao, Qing Dynasty, collection of Yangzhou Museum

These classical painters worked with lines rather than opaque pigments and shadowing, techniques prevalent in classical art in the West. Literati penjing followed such a tradition, using line as a means to render poetic beauty. The upright line conveys ruggedness, vigor and solemnity, while a curvy one suggests subtlety and idyllic beauty (fig. 31). A bold line signifies majestic force while a thin one, aloof elegance. A penjing artist infuses his or her own idiosyncratic design with passion and aspiration, through linear structures suggesting rhythm, character and elegance (fig. 32).

Variations of line are important to penjing design. A straight line can be accompanied by a curvy one to show a contrast of force and resilience, or the masculine and feminine. The varied lines in a fine penjing creation, each a unique masterstroke of art and nature, fuse into a balanced whole, imbuing mood and character in keeping with the Chinese aesthetic tradition (fig. 33).

Fig. 31 *Two Dragons over a Valley*
Species: Hedge sageretia (*Sageretia theezans*)
Spread: 100 cm
Age: 40 years
Designer: Han Xuenian
Introduction: This cliff-hanging penjing looks like two dragons swooping in over a deep valley, with varied lines of firmness and gentleness, and a force much like that in wild running calligraphy.

Fig. 32 *The Likeness of an Immortal*
Species: Chinese red pine (*Pinus massoniana*)
Height: 150 cm
Age: 60 years
Designer: Chen Chang
Introduction: The varied lines create a pleasing rhythm, stressing both contrasts and balance between the thick and lean, dense and sparse, and curvy and straight.

Fig. 33 *Striking Energy*
Species: Chinese elm (*Ulmus parvifolia*)
Height: 90 cm
Age: 40 years
Designer: Wu Chengfa
Introduction: This literati style penjing shows steely lines. The two upright trunks, with upper branches cascading from on high, produce a striking effect of contrasts.

Fig. 34 *Lone Angler on a Wintry River* by Ma Yuan, Southern Song period, collection of Tokyo National Museum. With a lone skiff and sparing lines to denote waves, the space and emptiness in the painting leave much room for the viewer's imagination. Its stark minimalism conveys a poetic image of the immensity of the river.

Fig. 35 Empty space in Qi Baishi's painting of his iconic river shrimps denotes water and reflected sky.

Fig. 36 *Panache*
Species: Taiwan juniper (*Juniperus formosana*)
Height: 100 cm
Age: 40 years
Designer: Zheng Zhilin
Introduction: A lean and aloof tree, with sparse limbs and foliage, this penjing demonstrates refined elegance, with empty spaces inspiring imagination.

3. Space

A lean, trim look with iconic simplicity is characteristic of literati penjing. These works are appreciated for such artful, simple and unencumbered elegance. A literati penjing can be seen as a three-dimensional rendition of a classical Chinese painting. It creates a stronger sense of space than other types of penjing.

The use of empty space and spare form creates aesthetic impact through a contrast between denseness and sparseness, and solid and void. In a painting a void has a structural meaning; both the painted areas and blank spaces are important. The spaces filled by ink and the whiteness of the void create dramatic tension.

In the words of Dai Xi (1801–1860), a Qing Dynasty painter, "An image is modeled through brush and ink, yet its aesthetic appeal is evidenced by the void." The emptiness leaves room for unbound imagination. A noted example of this technique is *Lone Angler on a Wintry River* by Ma Yuan of the Southern Song Dynasty (fig. 34). Qi Baishi was known for his vivid renditions of swimming shrimp, without actually painting the water. The blank space in his painting serves not only a structural purpose but also as a statement of meaning (fig. 35).

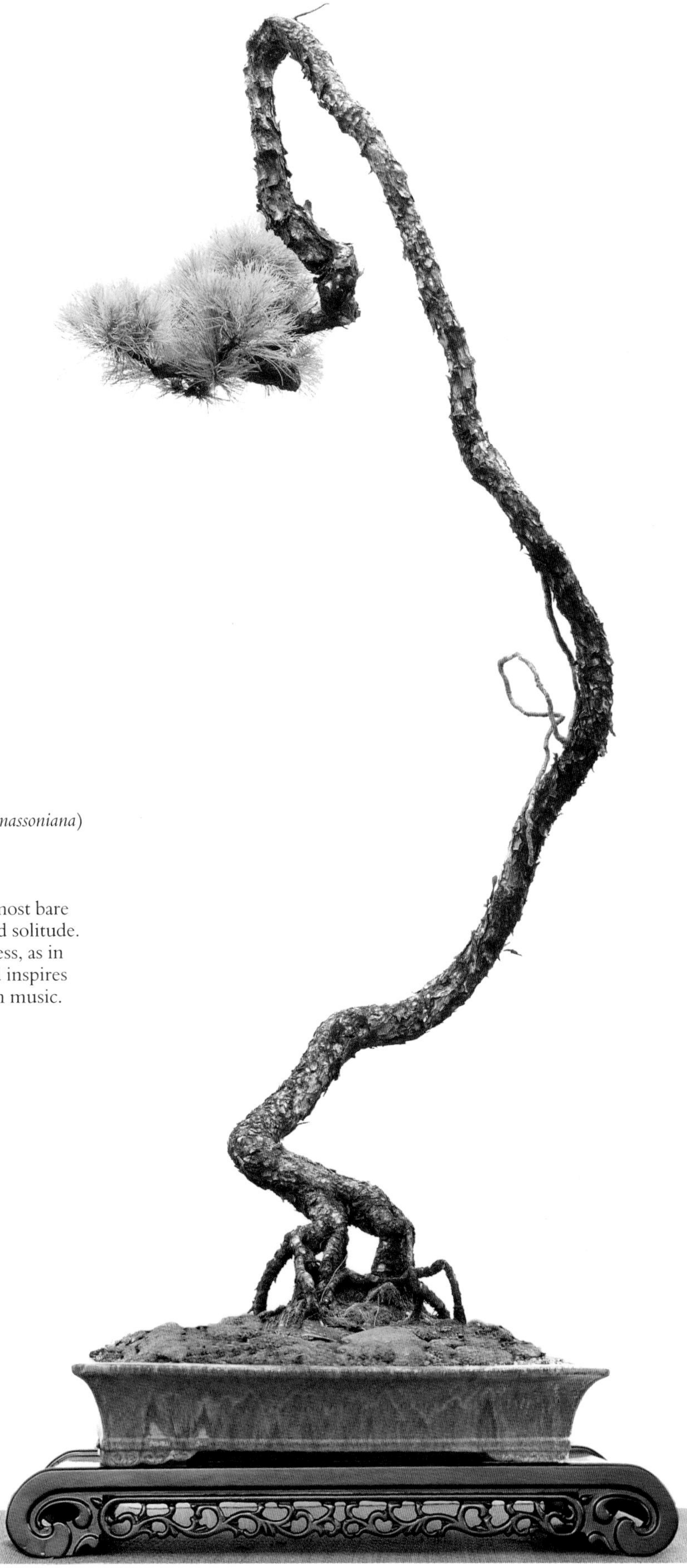

Fig. 37 *Silent Solitude*
Species: Chinese red pine (*Pinus massoniana*)
Height: 150 cm
Age: 30 years
Designer: Han Xuenian
Introduction: The lone trunk, almost bare of twigs, has an air of aloofness and solitude. It creates an eerie sense of emptiness, as in a traditional Chinese painting, and inspires imagination like a dramatic hold in music.

Fig. 38 *Exploring in Mist*
Species: Chinese red pine (*Pinus massoniana*)
Spread: 125 cm
Age: 30 years
Designer: Han Xuenian
Introduction: This cliff-hanging penjing, with its trunk reaching down beyond the rim of the pot, portrays resilience and freedom along with vigor and poise.

Void defines the solid. Blank space is not nothingness; it signifies inner essence and beauty, in a penjing as well as with a dramatic pause in music or during a theater performance. In silence, energy and character shine through (figs. 36, 37).

Such use of space in literati penjing follows a minimalist approach. Foliage is often trimmed to the minimum, leaving very sparse or no limbs at all on the lower trunk. The top can be pruned further back than with other types of penjing, contributing to an air of "proud loneliness" (fig. 38).

Such simplicity cannot be equaled to a lack of sophistication. Using this simplicity and rejecting opacity, the artist aims to capture the inner essence and sophisticated character of the subject. In simplicity lies elegance and taste. These qualities, though hard to attain, are made possible by a mastery of techniques and distillation of concrete images. A literati penjing, challenging to a novice, requires a well-honed sense of judgment and cultural sophistication, as well as technical achievement and meticulous efforts.

The spatial beauty of the literati penjing is achieved through a balance of denseness and sparseness. While a tightly-packed specimen, losing its aloofness, may make the viewer feel uneasy and even depressed, one that is too sparse feels loose and shapeless, lacking in spirit. Properly maintained contrasts create inner rhythm in a penjing, imbuing it with force and music. Less is more.

There are no prescribed rules regarding density in any literati penjing. Aside from inherent natural qualities, you should be guided by your own judgment. This contributes to the unique character of each work. As a rule of thumb, you should err on the sparse side.

Ancient Chinese philosophers believed the universe is an interplay of void and matter. Such a belief has also influenced traditional Chinese art, as we have seen, demonstrated through the use of space and blankness in all its disciplines: poetry, literature, drama, dance, music, painting, calligraphy and horticulture.

In designing literati penjing, the focus should be on the balance between formal opposites: trunk and limbs, foliage and space, plant and soil/pot. This creates contrast and nuance through the interplay of solid and void (figs. 39, 40).

Literati penjing are thus akin to poetry, composed with sparing brushstrokes, potent with meaning. As an art form, not an exact and explicit science, literati penjing can be inspiring with its subtle notes and evocative powers.

Fig. 39 *Upright Pine and Willowy Grace*
Species: Chinese red pine (*Pinus massoniana*)
Height: 125 cm
Age: 30 years
Designer: Han Xuenian
Introduction: This specimen features a twisted trunk reaching upward and two branches dropping vertically from the apex. It conveys force and subtlety through contrasts between space and solidness, and spread and convergence.

Fig. 40 *Candor*
Species: Japanese black pine (*Pinus thunbergii*)
Height: 120 cm
Age: 40 years
Designer: Zheng Zhilin
Introduction: This twin-trunk composition, with a simple and bold structure, conveys a sense of candor and righteousness.

4. Poetic Imagery

An important device in Chinese aesthetics, poeticism derives from a) the representation of image, and b) the interpretation and infusion of emotion. The former is "concrete/solid" while the latter represents "intangible/void." Rather than straightforward likeness or representation, poetic imagery requires a union of the objective and subjective.

As in other literati pursuits, the ultimate goal of literati penjing is poetic beauty. A penjing artist imbues emotion into physical recreations of scenery, like the landscape poet does with words. The artist strives to convey meaning with miniature trees and rocks in a small container, which come together likes lines of a poem, inspiring emotional response from the viewer.

"That which satisfies the mind is superior to what is only pleasing to the eye." As Su Shi (1037–1101), the Song Dynasty (960–1279) painter, poet and statesman, said, "Anyone who judges painting by form-likeness shows merely the insight of a child; anyone who makes poetry following this pattern is not a true poet." Poetic imagery stimulates the mind, and allows us to view a work over and over again with fresh eyes, always discovering a new aspect and never feeling satiated.

While an image has form, poetic mood is ethereal. The poetic imagery of a penjing captures the intangible and extends beyond the confines of a potted scene. The imagery can be forceful, bold, restrained or delicate. Works of literati penjing, with their reliance on minimalism, display the qualities of aloofness, slenderness, simplicity and refined grace, with an aesthetic impact that evokes the force in tranquility and meaning in the void (fig. 41).

The key is to elicit the inner essence of the subject, giving it unique character by eliminating the superfluous and redundant. Such reductionism, pushed

Fig. 41 Chan *Enlightenment*
Species: Indian hawthorn (*Rhaphiolepis indica*)
Height: 120 cm
Age: 15 years
Designer: Wu Chengfa
Introduction: The utterly lean and aloof trunk portrays the uncompromising character of a man of culture. The primary branch drops dramatically, pointing to the miniature of an old sage. Such an image makes one ponder the virtue of acceptance and otherworldliness.

Fig. 42 *Mist-Veiled Water*
Species: Waxy leaf privet (*Ligustrum quihoui*) and pomegranate (*Punica granatum*)
Type of rock: Turtle shell rock
Length of container: 100 cm
Age: 8 years (main tree)
Designer: Zhao Qingquan
Introduction: This water-and-land penjing was inspired by a line from a poem by Cui Hao (d. 754): "The mist-veiled waves of River Han make me homesick." The rocky landscape represents substance in contrast to the empty sky and fluid void. Yet emptiness and substance only exist in relation to each other. This is the kind of poetic state touted by the Qing Dynasty painter Da Chongguang (1623–1692).

to the extreme (for example an absurdly slim trunk and extremely shallow pot), in fact helps make poetic imagery authentic and powerfully evocative. To capture "the void in solid," carefully-created spaces are so designed to give expression and meaning to the artist's aspirations and sensibility (fig. 42).

Imagery and association are oft-used devices. Literati painters of old injected meaning into everyday subjects, such as the pine, bamboo and plum blossom, referring to them as the "three companions in winter." They became symbolic of a man of culture: hardy as an evergreen pine in winter (fig. 43), aloof as unbending bamboo, and noble as a blossoming plum defying winter cold. While the art of literati penjing often aims to portray traits like these, different species have varied associations, inspiring enlightenment through symbolism.

The names given to literati penjing projects also help elicit their symbolic significance, as does a painting's inscription or a plaque decorating a garden, bearing a literary name. Upon completing the styling of a penjing, giving it a name befitting its theme and poetic overtone enhances its aesthetic appeal and the viewer's appreciation. This is especially true of literati penjing. Naming should also follow the rules of simplicity and subtlety; those that convey a poetic sense as well as hinting of *Chan* are most highly regarded.

Facing page
Fig. 43 *A Noble Scholar*
Species: Five-needle pine (*Pinus parviflora*)
Height: 95 cm
Age: 32 years
Designer: Zhao Qingquan
Introduction: This pine, with an upright trunk and drooping branches, projects an unruffled poise and independence, symbolic of literati aspirations.

文化渊源

CHAPTER TWO
Cultural Origins

The art of Chinese penjing started chiefly as a pursuit of men of culture, the scholarly elite. Its practice, which shares common cultural origins with Chinese gardening, landscape painting and nature poetry, has been deeply influenced by the aesthetics of Chinese classical painting.

The art of literati penjing is thought to be the most representative of the scholar-artists' aesthetic aspirations. Although the term "literati penjing" gained currency only in modern times (because of the spread of the Japanese term *bunjin* with the same meaning), such an approach has existed in Chinese penjing since ancient times. Although it is difficult to pin down when the style first appeared, it is without doubt rooted in literati art and the philosophical traditions of ancient China: Confucianism, Taoism and *Chan*.

Fig. 44 *A Pine atop a Mountain Ridge*
Species: Five-needle pine (*Pinus parviflora*)
Height: 70 cm
Age: 35 years
Designer: Zhao Qingquan
Introduction: This literati penjing adopts an "overlooking-the-water" style. The five-needle pine has a shape that is well structured and simple but shows individuality. The trunk progresses toward the left, well beyond the container. This specimen captures what Huang Tingjian, a well-known poet of the Song Dynasty, wrote in one of his poems about the sound of the wind in pines atop a mountain ridge, which can be heard miles away.

1. Penjing and Literati Painting

While its origins can be traced back to the Han (206 BC–AD 220) and Jin (265–420) dynasties, penjing as an art form arose in China in the early Tang Dynasty. By the Song and Yuan (1271–1368) dynasties, the Chinese were already practicing the art at an advanced level. The Ming (1368–1644) and Qing dynasties saw the art form's peak before a decline in the following era. The conditions in China at present have allowed for a renaissance of this ancient art. As literati penjing initially evolved by drawing inspirations from literati painting, an understanding of the literati and their culture, as well as the concurrent development of penjing, can serve as a useful introduction.

Historical Overview

The Chinese began cultivating plants for their appealing beauty as early as the Yin Period (14th–11th century BC), building landscape gardens as representations of the natural world more than three thousand years ago. The famed *Shang Lin* Garden of the Qin Dynasty (221–206 BC) once covered an area spanning nearly one hundred miles at both its widest and longest. It was also recorded that people in the Eastern Han Dynasty (25–220) planted flowers in containers and collected rocks to create miniature mountains.

The Northern and Southern Dynasties (220–589) was a period of chaos and dynastic collapse. Learned men retreated into the natural world to find solace and sanctuary from the turmoil and rampant wars. To be able to appreciate the beauty of nature unbothered was their dream of an ideal life. They extolled the virtues of simplicity, refined elegance, reclusive existence and self-cultivation, which gained currency among scholar-officials and brought about the rise of landscape gardens, painting and poetry.

Zong Bing (375–443) theorized about landscape painting in his *Introduction to Landscape Painting*. He put forth the notion of "capturing the inner spirit through form-representation" and the "union of form and the essence," emphasizing that landscape painting was about conveying the inner landscape of the artist's heart and mind. Such a notion inspired artists to also create miniaturized landscapes in three-dimensions, using a pot or tray, as a means of creating beauty and expressing one's self.

The short-lived Sui Dynasty (581–618) saw the creation of the civil service examination. Starting in 605, the system lasted for thirteen centuries before its abolition in 1905. It affected the Chinese society in profound ways, creating a class of scholar-bureaucrats with cultural sophistication and elevated status. They are credited for starting the literati art tradition.

The Tang Dynasty was the golden age of Chinese poetry, painting and sculpture. Wang Wei (c. 701–761), a Tang poet and painter, is regarded by art historians as the earliest literati painter, although literati tendencies in paintings emerged in the earlier Northern and Southern Dynasties. His landscape paintings reflected inner realities and personality, with reference to *Chan*. He was also a penjing artist, known for his cultivated orchids in ceramic pots decorated with rocks of pleasing colors and fine texture.

During this period, penjing became an art form. Well-known poets and essayists indulged in its pursuit. Poets Du Fu (712–770) and Li He (790–816) both made references to penjing techniques in their poems. The fresco in the tomb of Prince Zhang Huai at the Qianling necropolis, dated to 706, shows maidservants carrying penjing.

Scholar-officials comprised an important social stratum in the Song Dynasty, representing the cultural elite. Poet, essayist and statesman Su Shi put forth the notion of the "scholar-painter," as opposed to the artisan painters, or craftsmen, who sought only lifelike representations.

Theories about literati painting also appeared as the practice became established. The artist Guo Xi (1023–c. 1085) noted, "Poetry is painting without form and painting poetry." Su Shi referred to "painting in poetry; poetry in painting." There were both proponents of literati art as a medium of self-expression, which allowed artists to capture the inner spirit of the subject rather than only its appearance. Literati painters added poems or literary inscriptions to their paintings to state their emotions and aspirations. Trees painted by such artists tended to be lean and haughty, which without doubt influenced penjing.

Facing page
Fig. 45 *Enlightenment*
Species: Chinese red pine (*Pinus massoniana*)
Height: 115 cm
Age: 50 years
Designer: Zheng Yongtai
Introduction: The aged-looking trunk reaches up and then bends back in a vertical drop, with cascading branches extending to the right. The dramatic composition shows weather-beaten maturity and age.

Fig. 46 *Dwarf Siberian Pine*, painting by Li Shixing, Yuan Dynasty

Fig. 47 Detail, *Spring Leisure Pursuit* by an unknown painter, Ming Dynasty, collection of Nanjing Museum

Fig. 48 *Wuling in Spring* by Wu Wei, Ming Dynasty, collection of Palace Museum, Beijing

The Yuan Dynasty (1271–1368) saw the flourishing of literati painting. The scholar-painters employed calligraphy and poetry in their paintings to assert their identity. Zhao Mengfu (1254–1322), whose works influenced a whole generation of practitioners, first proposed the new paradigm for the literati painter and the notion of painting grounded in calligraphy. This influenced penjing design at the time, as can be seen in the penjing depicted in the Yuan Dynasty painting *Dwarf Siberian Pine*, which displays characteristics of a literati penjing (fig. 46).

Dong Qichang (1555–1636) of the Ming Dynasty used the terms "southern" and "northern" to describe schools of contrasting styles, branding the former as literati and latter artisan. He was a staunch opponent of the northern school, which prized representation, and an advocate of the southern approach that emphasized the inner essence. His efforts greatly promoted literati painting to the cultural mainstream. The art of penjing also thrived in this period. *Spring Leisure Pursuit* (fig. 47) and *Wuling in Spring* (fig. 48), both paintings from the period, depict two fine examples of literati penjing that embody a high level of sophistication.

Fig. 49 *Companionship*
Species: Five-needle pine (*Pinus parviflora*)
Height: 95 cm
Age: 32 years
Designer: Zhao Qingquan
Introduction: A twin-trunk composition with the upright primary trunk having an apex slanting toward right and a curvy secondary trunk inclining in the same direction, displaying contrast, reconciliation and stylistic cohesion.

Fig. 50 *Landscape* by Ma Yuan, Song Dynasty, collection of Palace Museum, Taipei

Fig. 51 Detail, *Early Spring* by Guo Xi, Song Dynasty, collection of Palace Museum, Taipei

Fig. 52 *Pine and Rocks* by Sheng Zizhao, Yuan Dynasty, collection of Palace Museum, Beijing

Tu Long (1543–1605) wrote in his *Desultory Remarks on Furnishing the Abode of the Retired Scholar* about book editions, calligraphy masterpieces, prized writing paper, ink slabs and stones, paintings and zithers, with comments on penjing. The definitive work on the aesthetics of the scholar-artist was later brought to Japan and "became much sought after and came out in a printed edition in 1803 after hand-copied versions fell short of popular demand. It became a requisite in any Japanese scholar's study and its chapter on *pen wan* ('potted plaything') had a significant impact on scholars at the time." ("A Study on Literati—the Past, Present and Future of the Scholar-Artist and Literati Bonsai," *Modern Bonsai Journal*, No. 2, 2004, Japan.)

Tu Long also commented on the extensive borrowing by penjing artists of the poetic images found in paintings. He noted, "The most elegant specimens conveying a sense of antiquity are foot-tall and inch-thick *Tianmu* pines with fine, short needles, their slanting form evoking paintings by Ma Yuan (fig. 50), towering apex those by Guo Xi (fig. 51), flowing grace those by Sheng Zizhao (fig. 52) and cascading force those by Liu Songnian (fig. 53). Grown in fine pots, they offer a varied and striking sight."

Fig. 53 *Reading by the Window in Autumn* by Liu Songnian, Song Dynasty, collection of Liaoning Provincial Museum

The specimens mentioned in the book are mostly lean, tall, plain, elegant and aloof. The Tianmu pine is in fact the Taiwan pine (*Pinus taiwanensis*) that grows at Tianmu Mountain in Zhejiang Province. Because of the harsh habitat, they are dwarf-sized with short needles, grow very slowly and are ideal for literati penjing (fig. 54).

The Qing Dynasty produced a number of accomplished literati painters, most notably Shi Tao (1641–c. 1718), Zhu Da (c. 1626–1705), Kun Can (1612–1692) and Hong Ren (1610–1664), known as the "Four Monk Painters," who had far-reaching

Fig. 54 *A Pine in Lingnan*
Species: Chinese red pine (*Pinus massoniana*)
Height: 135 cm
Age: 40 years
Designer: Han Xuenian
Introduction: With sparse foliage, these two trunks with the same root system contrast in size. Simply structured, the work is thought-provoking.

Fig. 55 *Chinese Plum Penjing* by Wang Tubing, Qing Dynasty, collection of Palace Museum, Taipei

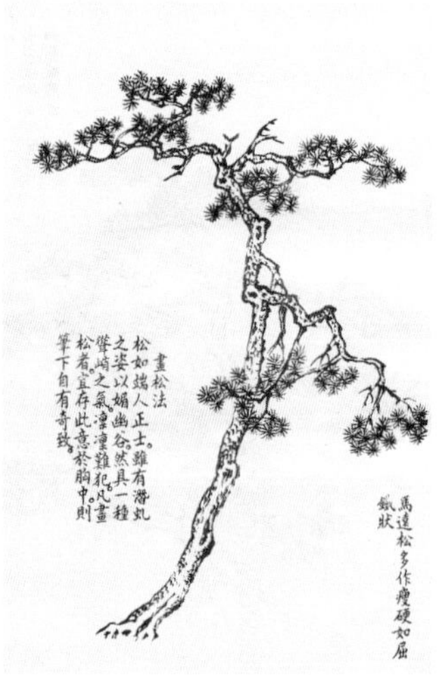

Fig. 56 Pine depicted in *The Mustard Seed Garden Painting Manual*

Fig. 57 *Verdant Agedness* (Chinese box, *Murraya paniculata*), penjing specimen by Su Ren

influences on later artists. Penjing also achieved unprecedented popularity, with more styles and regional variations. Artists explored the use of a wider variety of materials, and publications on the art form proliferated, of which *Designing Penjing* by Chen Haozi and *On Penjing* by Su Ling were thought to be most influential. The painting *Chinese Plum Penjing* by Wang Tubing (1668–1743) shows a style popular at the time (fig. 55).

The Mustard Seed Garden Painting Manual, published in 1679 and the first manual for Chinese painting, became a popular guide for enthusiasts of literati penjing as well (fig. 56). In fact the book not only left an indelible mark on Chinese penjing, but also on the evolution of literati bonsai in Japan. Japanese bonsai artists emulated "the style of refined elegance of Chinese literati" and paid "homage to textbook models of southern school literati art as seen in depictions of pines in *The Mustard Seed Garden Painting Manual*." ("A Study on Literati—the Past, Present and Future of the Scholar-Artist and Literati Bonsai," *Modern Bonsai Journal*, No. 2, 2004, Japan.)

Around the end of the Qing Dynasty, treatises of greater intellectual depth on literati painting came forth, the most notable of which was an essay by Chen Shizeng (1876–1923) entitled *The Value of Literati Painting*. He wrote, "A literati painting is judged by its essential qualities reflecting the scholar-artist's ideals and sophistication, rather than its technical attributes; by its literati sentiments beyond the painted image." He further commented, "A literati painting is valued for its conveying the inner essence rather than form-likeness. Therefore, a literati painting may have merit in spite of formal pitfalls. There are fine examples of literati paintings that may be otherwise regarded as unbeautiful, eccentric, rough and overly bold. Yet they are nonetheless valued, precisely because of their simplicity as opposed to decoration, plainness to prettiness, and eccentricity to conformity. For only in such works beyond contrivance and pretension, moral quality and character shine through. Literati paintings in this vein are to be viewed with admiration and awe."

With the demise of the Qing Dynasty came the decline of Chinese penjing. There were a few notable exceptions. Penjing specimens created by the monk Su Ren (1894–1962) of the Hai Tong Monastery in Guangzhou were noted for their aloof character and *Chan*-like stark simplicity. The style attributed to him bears his name to this day. His tree specimens, though similar in some ways to other literati penjing, have much leaner trunks and sparse foliage, true to his adage, "Perfection can be diminished by one twig too many or too few." His is an extreme approach to literati penjing (fig. 57).

Given Western cultural influences, the spread of education and technology, and division of labor, a modern-day person of culture is a far cry from the literati of old. The literati as a class exists no more. But the ideals they once represented are still relevant and find expression in Chinese art.

Chinese penjing began a renaissance in the 1970s, as innovative techniques were being experimented with and new designs created, demonstrating a tendency of growing individuality. In this context, literati penjing as a means of self-expression has gained greater popularity (fig. 58).

Fig. 58 *Nobleness*
Species: Sargent's juniper (*Juniperus chinensis var. sargentii*)
Height: 115 cm
Age: 30 years
Designer: Zhao Qingquan
Introduction: This juniper, with its lean, upright trunk and drooping branches, projects unruffled poise and independence, emblematic of literati aspirations.

Fig. 59 *Twin Trees in Lingnan*
Species: June snow (*Serissa foetita*)
Height: 80 cm
Age: 40 years
Designer: Han Xuenian
Introduction: This literati piece was inspired by the style of Su Ren. Its lean twin-trunks with sparing branches and foliage portray an image of poise, detachment and self-assuredness, with refreshing minimalism.

Fig. 60 *Chinese Plum, Rock Creek and Waterfowl* by Ma Yuan, Song Dynasty, collection of Palace Museum, Beijing

Fig. 61 *Mist-Veiled Mountain Valley, Cottage and Trees* by Xia Gui, Song Dynasty, collection of Palace Museum, Beijing

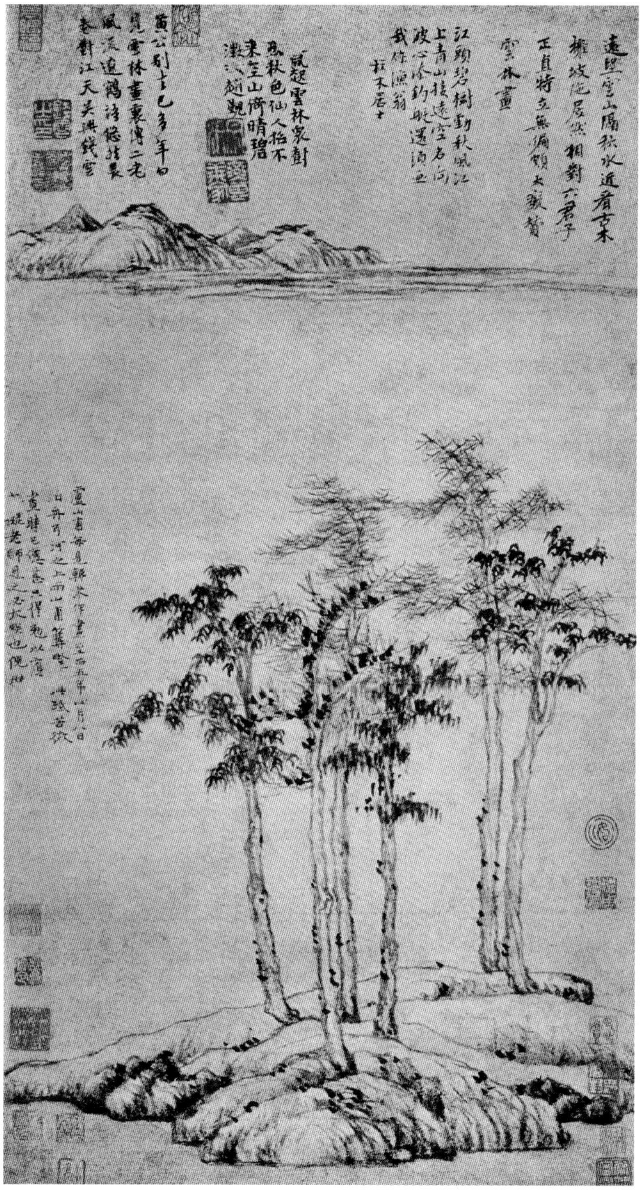

Fig. 62 *Six Noblemen* by Ni Yunlin, Yuan Dynasty, collection of Shanghai Museum

Common Characteristics

As we have seen the art of literati penjing mirrors the defining characteristics of literati painting, with an emphasis on self-expression more than formal representation.

Literati painting celebrates an unattached individuality. Being cultivated men, the scholar-painters strived to be free from conventions and projected an uncompromising spirit in their paintings. Aloofness is also a defining feature of literati penjing, with slender, upright trunks and sparing branches toward the apex. There is invariable ruggedness about the upright trunk, conveying an unyielding spirit, a hallmark of the literati. Even with twin- or multi-trunk or forest style designs, each trunk displays literati features on its own, while collectively forming a coherent whole (fig. 59).

Literati painting is also marked by an economy of means, keeping only what is absolutely necessary and leaving blank spaces suggesting what lies beyond representation. Such use of imperfect form affords effective expression, as seen in landscape paintings by Ma Yuan and Xia Gui of the Southern Song Dynasty. These feature a so-called "one-corner" style, with the bulk of composition confined to only one corner or on one side, leaving the rest of the field more or less empty (works of Ma: fig. 60 and of Xia: fig. 61). Another example is Ni Yunlin (1306 or 1301–1374), whose paintings of distant rocky hills with lonely trees, rendered with economy, were of lasting appeal (fig. 62). Such economy is also evident in fine literati penjing, with branches and foliage pruned back to the minimum to give the effect of "the world in a twig or leaf."

Fig. 63 *A Pine Extraordinaire*
Species: Five-needle pine (*Pinus parviflora*)
Height: 70 cm
Age: 35 years
Designer: Zhao Qingquan
Introduction: Inspired by Song Dynasty master Ma Yuan's iconic asymmetry, the composition shows an outstretching trunk with branches and foliage all in the upper quadrant. This places the center of gravity seemingly outside the pot, creating space beyond conventional boundaries, and projects stark simplicity and aloofness.

Artlessness is valued most highly in literati painting. Rejecting color pigments, literati painters worked with ink and wash. Their interest in the projection of inner essence, going beyond form-likeness and artifice, became a defining feature of literati penjing. Simplicity, being free from artifice, was most valued, as opposed to decoration and frivolousness, which violate the law of nature. Penjing specimens adopting such an approach show naturalness and flowing elegance (fig. 63).

Self-cultivation was essential to literati painting. The art evolved from a union of scholarship and calligraphy. The brushwork practiced in calligraphy was the basis of ink-brush painting. The lines and ink dots took on aesthetic appeal to the scholar-painters. Literati penjing likewise features pronounced lines, not merely as structural elements but as expressions of emotion and inner vision.

Literati penjing are thus a mode of self-expression. You may see vastly different works created by designers living in the same age because of their distinctive personalities and emotional responses. They may display, in highly personalized idioms, aloofness, simplicity, integrity and self-assurance against the worldliness and greed in society. Cultivating literati penjing is seen as a way of character building and educating oneself, as well in Japan, and has been gaining popularity in the West too. Literati penjing with minimalist tendencies can even be seen as in line with some branches of modern art.

2. Philosophical Traditions

The evolution of literati penjing has been influenced by Chinese philosophical traditions. They include Confucianism, with its emphasis on self-cultivation; Taoism, with is focus on serenity and the mystic void; and the simplicity and minimalism of *Chan*. These traditions have shaped the expression, aesthetics and criteria of literati penjing.

Confucianism

The teachings by Confucius (551–479 BC), which emphasize harmony between man and nature and universal benevolence, held a place of preeminence and orthodoxy in ancient China. His notion of the ideal man is man of cultivation.

The *Analects*, a record of his teachings, includes such sayings as: "The wise find joy in water, the benevolent in mountains," advocating education and enlightenment through closeness to nature; and: "Only in winter do we appreciate that the pine and cypress are the last to fade," extolling resilience and uprightness.

Literati paintings often portray the Chinese plum, orchid, bamboo and chrysanthemum, four iconic plants representing qualities of the ideal person. Another common subject is the "three companions in winter," the hardy pine, bamboo and Chinese plum. Literati penjing sought similar projection of personality, choosing pine and juniper for their symbolic qualities.

The Confucian ideal of artlessness and simplicity ("the highest style of music is distinguished by its ease; of elegance, by its simplicity") also finds expression in literati penjing. Masterful specimens are marked by their spare foliage and stark simplicity, with an air of aloofness (fig. 64).

Fig. 64 *Companionship*
Species: *Erythrophleum fordii oliv*
Height: 95 cm
Age: 20 years
Designer: Zheng Yongtai
Introduction: Simply structured, the lean twin-trunk composition with stark twigs and minimal foliage creates space and openness that inspire imagination.

Following the Confucian tenet of moderation, scholar-artists sought refined elegance and balance, employing nuanced, economical brushwork. Literati penjing followed the same principle to achieve balance between formal opposites: the primary and secondary, top and base, firmness and gentleness, and denseness and sparseness (figs. 65, 66).

Art criticism of old often referred to moral quality and character in paintings. Refined elegance, magnanimity, gentleness and a sense of justice underscored classical Chinese art. Personal character had a direct bearing on art, as stated in the famous work, *The Mustard Seed Garden Painting Manual*: "Pine trees are like people of high principles whose manner reveals an inner power. They resemble dragons coiled in deep gorges; they have an attractive, graceful air, yet one trembles to approach them for fear of the hidden power ready to spring forth. Those who paint pine trees should keep this in mind. The brush will then effortlessly produce extraordinary results." (*The Mustard Seed Garden Painting Manual*, Transl. Ed. by Mai-mai Sze, Princeton University Press, NY, 1956, p101)

Fig. 65 *Pine Whisper on Moonlit Night*
Species: Japanese black pine (*Pinus thunbergii*)
Height: 76 cm
Age: 40 years
Designer: Xu Hao
Introduction: These two trunks with the same root system contrast well in size and possess a stately elegance. A pine is emblematic of the noble gentleman, a literati ideal.

Fig. 66 *Moderation*
Species: Five-needle pine (*Pinus parviflora*)
Height: 110 cm
Age: 40 years
Designer: Zheng Zhilin
Introduction: The tall, dominant trunk is complimented by the short secondary trunk, with the stooping posture of the former echoed by the latter. Exhibiting a fine balance of opposites, it evokes a sense of the golden mean central to Confucianism.

Taoism

As one of the three major belief systems in ancient China, Taoism was a great source of inspiration for Chinese art, with a profound impact on literature, painting, landscape gardening and penjing. The art of Chinese penjing owes much to Taoist aesthetics for some of its unique characteristics.

Taoism is centered principally on the teachings of the ancient thinkers Laozi (c. 570–470 BC) of the Spring and Autumn Period (770–476 BC), and Zhuangzi (c. 369–286 BC). Laozi describes the *Dao* (or *Tao*) as the source of all existence, and urges a return to nature and the state of *wu wei*, or being free from desires. Zhuangzi inherited Laozi's philosophical tradition and took it a step further in his pursuit of absolute spiritual freedom. He believed "the universe has great beauty yet it says nothing," and advocated harmony with nature as well as action that is not based on motives for gain.

Fig. 67 *Majestic Form*
Species: Hedge sageretia (*Sageretia theezans*)
Height: 150 cm
Age: 60 years
Designer: Wu Chengfa
Introduction: With an upright main trunk and outstretching first branch, the design demonstrates elegant force and natural poise. The demure secondary trunk contrasts with the aloofness of the main trunk and its sense of bold integrity.

Taoism values naturalness, minimalism, ethereal beauty and serenity, and it is void of exploitative motives and flows with nature, all of which are attributes sought in literati penjing (fig. 67).

Harmony between man and nature is quintessential Taoism. In nature there is equilibrium, perfection and consummate beauty. The art of literati penjing aims to emulate nature through ardent abstraction. This approach bars clever artifice and extravagance. Naturalness is achieved through simplicity and spontaneity. This applies to styling and training as well, as the natural tendencies of the plant are sought and accommodated, be it an upright pine, a rugged juniper, an elegant weeping willow or a graceful maple.

Minimalism is key to Taoist aesthetics. Laozi said, "*Dao* lies in utter simplicity; the greatest sounds are not audible; and the greatest beauty has no form." Also: "More is confusion; less is gain." This aesthetic approach has influenced poetry, painting and prose in China since antiquity. The stylistic simplicity of literati penjing engendered by such tradition can be both pleasing and enlightening, eliciting contemplations on the meaning of life and universal energy.

"Being in tune with nature, manifesting plainness and having few desires" is an adage that is deeply rooted in Taoism, which urges people to reduce selfishness and embrace simplicity in attempting spiritual transcendence. The best literati paintings are valued for such simplicity, which rejects grandeur, and for naturalness. This type of simplicity informed by Taoism is also most prized in literati penjing, and serves as a guide for presentation, even including the choice of pots, trays and frames (fig. 68).

Fig. 68 *Out of Mountain Recesses*
Species: Sargent's juniper (*Juniperus chinensis var. sargentii*)
Height: 90 cm
Age: 30 years
Designer: Zhou Qijin
Introduction: The twisting trunk and curvy branches create flowing lines, with the lone left twig showing sharp contrast to the upper branches and foliage. The design, suggesting destiny and effortlessness, was inspired by a line from the poem *Oh, Homebound I Go*! by Tao Yuanming of the Jin Dynasty: "… the clouds idle away from their mountain recesses / without intent or purpose."

Fig. 69 *No Dust Fall*
Species: Chinese hackberry (*Celtis sinensis*)
Height: 165 cm
Age: 15 years
Designer: Han Xuenian
Introduction: The towering twin-trunk composition, with a few bare stubs toward the top, is utterly simple and pure, true to the sentiments in the poem by Hui Neng, the Sixth Patriarch of *Chan* Buddhism: "Bodhi is not any tree / Mirror is no stand. / Where void prevails / How could dust fall?"

Chan

As a sect of Buddhism that came into prominence during the Tang Dynasty, *Chan* (Zen) was thought to have been derived from teachings of the Buddha, transmitted to Mahakasyapa, one of his principle disciples, and brought into China by the sixth-century monk Bodhidharma, who was regarded as the sect's first patriarch in China. It gained greater currency because of the practice of Hui Neng (638–713), a Chinese monk viewed as the sect's sixth patriarch.

Chinese philosophical thinking also shaped the evolution of this form of Buddhism, infusing into it Taoist and Confucian notions. *Chan* came into the mainstream of Chinese thought and was the type of Buddhism favored by scholar-officials. Its tenets include: "wordlessness," "teach not to the uninitiated," and "point directly to the mind and perceive the true nature of Buddha through sudden enlightenment."

Chan became an approach to life, a way of thinking rather than merely a faith. It speaks to the heart and soul by inspiring authenticity and epiphany, and urges meditation with a "pure and unattached mind." Meditation is essential to sudden enlightenment, resulting in the insight that all living beings and nature are one; and that man is part of the universe, yet the mind is capable of covering the whole universe. The *Chan* is without form and beyond definition, and is achieved only through sudden insight.

Because of its focus on philosophical musing, sudden enlightenment, "wordlessness," solitude, aloofness and ascetic self-cultivation, *Chan* Buddhism became an intellectual magnet to men of culture who yearned to commune with nature. In the enlightened state, "The green mountain is *Chan*; the boundless land is *Chan*; the mighty Yangtze River is *Chan*; the murmuring stream is *Chan*; the green bamboo is *Chan*; the yellow flower is *Chan*; the starlit sky is *Chan*; the bright moon is *Chan*; the scorching sun is *Chan*; the gentle breeze is *Chan*; the pure white snow is *Chan*; and the drizzling rain is *Chan*."

The influence of *Chan* can be found in Chinese poetry, calligraphy, painting and gardening. Many of its devotees, painters in particular, imbued their artistic expressions with *Chan* insights. An understanding of *Chan* is hence indispensable to a deeper appreciation of Chinese art.

The *Chan* sect began its rise in the Tang Dynasty and became a powerful intellectual force in the succeeding Song period, leaving its mark on the evolution of Chinese penjing, the literati style in particular. Because of their signature aloofness, simplicity, plainness and ethereal grace, which match *Chan* ideals, literati penjing are sometimes called *Chan* trees. The imperfect form of the lean trunk and sparse foliage is almost quintessential *Chan*, which shuns extravagance that undermines focus on inner essence. Seeming imperfection inspires insight into the otherwise-elusive meaning of existence (figs. 69, 70).

Chan qualities in works of Chinese penjing give them a quality of poetic beauty, expanding their aesthetic possibilities, creating boundless beauty in a small pot. The cultivation of literati penjing informed by *Chan* ideals is a path to wisdom and the immense joy of enlightenment.

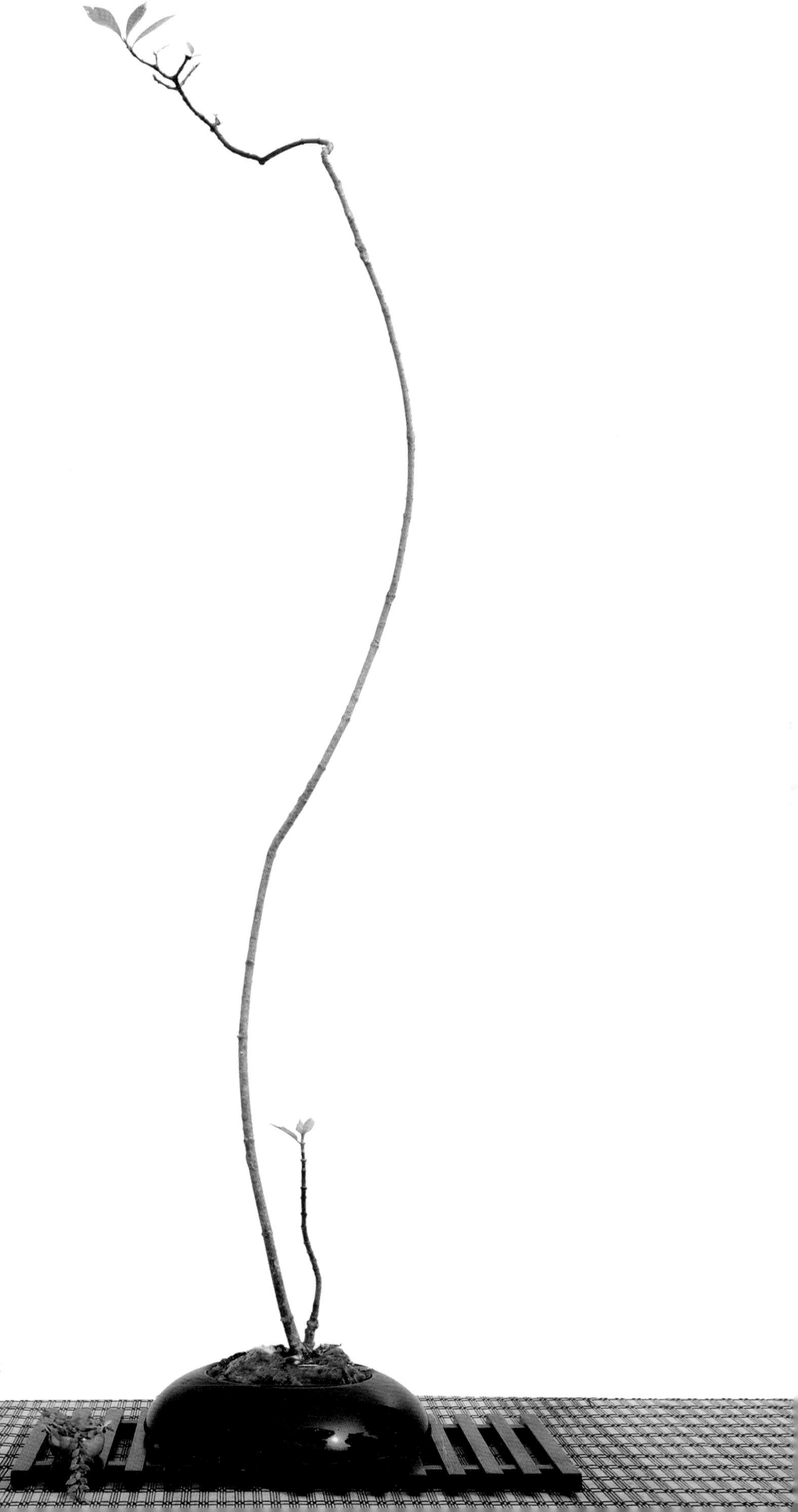

Fig. 70 *Effusiveness Gone*
Species: Cape jasmine (*Gardenia jasminoides Ellis*)
Height: 135 cm
Age: 5 years old
Designer: Han Xuenian
Introduction: This composition in Su Ren's signature style, has extremely lean twin trunks and a bare minimum of twigs and foliage. Such an imperfect form verges on the absurd and surreal but has the power to speak to the viewer's heart.

准备

CHAPTER THREE
Basic Techniques

Penjing is a practical art that can never be learned from books alone. Any success is the result of repeated practice and knowledge acquired through the use of various tools, as well as learning the characteristics of various species. In addition, one must master the techniques for propagating, growing, training and caring for penjing plants.

This chapter also covers elements of designing literati penjing. While it is easy to emulate certain compositions bearing literati features, it is always a challenge to create a true literati penjing, which requires both technical and cultural sophistication. There is simply no shortcut. To borrow the words of an eleventh-century Chinese author commenting on the poems of his contemporaries: "They look ordinary and yet are most marvelous / They appear easily done but require much assiduity." Upright character, knowledge and refinement are essential qualities in a literati penjing master.

Fig. 71 *Gorgeous Flowers*
Species: Azalea (*Rhododendron simsii*)
Height: 46 cm
Age: 40 years
Designer: Zhao Qingquan
Introduction: Azalea is a popular penjing species for its gorgeous flowers. This specimen has been trained from a shrub with several trunks. The unwanted trunks were removed, leaving one trunk and its whole root system, to fully display its beauty.

1. Trees, Pots and Soil

Trees, pots and soil are the three key elements in the composition of a literati penjing.

Source Trees

An ideal source tree for literati penjing should have sufficient branches placed toward the top, with an elongated trunk and rugged bark that bears the mark of age. The lines should be strong and smooth. Tree trunks that are too short and thick should be avoided.

Tree species are also selected for their symbolic qualities. Often chosen are the five-needle pine, Japanese black pine, Japanese red pine, Taiwan pine, Sargent's juniper, Taiwan juniper and Japanese yew. Littleleaf box and Chinese box are also used because of their slow growth rate, hard wood and longevity.

The species most often used for literati penjing cultivation in China include those in the table.

Pinus parviflora	Five-needle pine
Pinus taiwanensis	Taiwan pine
Pinus thunbergii	Japanese black pine
Pinus thunbergii var. corticosa	Brocaded pine
Pinus densiflora	Japanese red pine
Podocarpus macrophyllus	Japanese yew
Podocarpus macrophyllus var. maki	Shrubby yew
Juniperus chinensis var. sargentii	Sargent's juniper
Juniperus formosana	Taiwan juniper
Cupressus funebris	Chinese weeping cypress
Sabina procumbens	Procumbent juniper
Cryntomeria japonica	Japanese cedar
Taxodium distichum	Common bald cypress
Taxus cuspidata var. umbrcaulifera	Low Japanese yew
Ulmus parvifolia	Chinese elm
Sageretia theezans	Hedge sageretia
Celtis sinensis	Chinese hackberry
Buxus sinica	Littleleaf box (littleleaf boxwood)
Murraya paniculata	Chinese box (orange jasmine)
Poilaniella fragilis	Airy shaw
Tamarix chinensis	Chinese tamarisk
Ligustrum quihoui	Waxy leaf privet
Vitex negundo	Five-leaved chaste tree
Fraxinus chinensis	Chinese ash
Acer palmatum	Japanese maple
Ginkgo biloba	Maidenhair tree
Prunus mume	Chinese plum
Rhododendron simsii	Azalea
Chaenomeles speciosa	Flowering quince
Serissa foetita	June snow
Loropetalum chinense var. rubrum	Chinese fringe flower
Punica granatum	Pomegranate
Diospyros rhombifolia	Diamond-leaf persimmon
Pyracantha fortuneana	Firethorn

Containers

Round sandy clay pot

Round glazed pottery pot

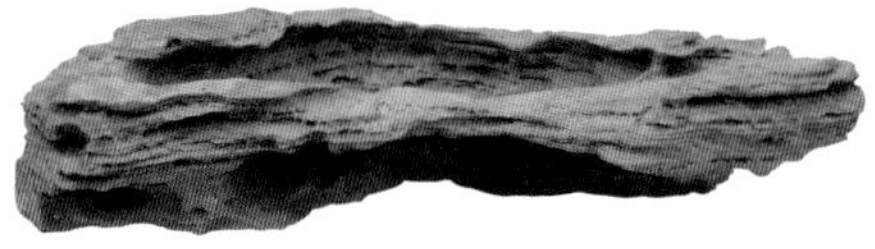

Natural stone container

Natural looking pottery tray

Pottery trays of irregular shapes

Fig. 72 Containers

Containers

While pots or trays are necessary in penjing for holding the plants, they are also a crucial part of your whole design (fig. 72).

Penjing pots of various colors and shapes are available in sandy clay ware, glazed pottery or porcelain. They can also be carved out of rock and made from a piece of stone in its natural shape. You can choose from this assortment the right pot to match the tree species. For example the rustic and earthy tone of sandy clay pots are perfect foils for green pines and junipers, while glazed pottery with a bright colored sheen is often used for shrubby plants.

The shape of containers for literati penjing can vary from round, which is most often used, to those shaped like a Chinese crabapple, round-petal whorl-shaped to hexagonal. Sometimes oval or rectangular pots may be favored. Natural stone slabs and natural looking pottery containers are suitable for all trees and plants.

As a rule of thumb, shallow pots are preferred for literati trees, except for the cliff-hanging style. The principle of simplicity should also apply here; with an antique feel and fine finish preferred, and lavish color, pattern or calligraphic engravings shunned.

Soil

Peat

Pine bark

Silica sand

Fig. 73 Soil

Soil

A literati penjing is confined to a relatively small space, in a shallow pot with sparse soil for its root system. Therefore it needs sufficient water, air and nutrition. Proper soil condition is essential for its good health. Many factors contribute to a good soil mix:

Water-retention. The soil needs to be able to hold and retain sufficient quantities of water and nutrients to supply the penjing.

Drainage. Excess water must be able to drain quickly from the pot. Soil lacking good drainage is prone to compaction or becoming soggy, leading to damage of the root system and plant death.

Aeration. The particles in a penjing soil mix should allow tiny gaps or air pockets between them. It is important to the health of the roots that they have access to oxygen, while enough bacteria are needed to decompose fertilizers so that plants can absorb nutrients.

Proper pH value. Tree species vary in their requirements for water and nutrients, which should be accommodated for in soil preparation. Soils can be subacid or slightly alkaline. As a rule the pH value should be kept between 6 and 7.5.

Soil mixes can be either organic or inorganic. Dead plant matter such as peat and composted leaves and bark can be organic soil components, which contain nutrients but may also suffer compaction. Inorganic soil mixes contain little or no organic matter; instead, they are made up of specially formulated soils such as silica sand, weathered granite, calcined (baked) or fired clays. The advantage of inorganic materials is that they hold their open structure for a long time. Pines, for instance, prefer inorganic soil mixes, while deciduous species are usually planted in organic mixes. There is no single soil mix that is best for cultivating penjing; variables such as local soil types, climate and tree species all contribute to the need for variations in one's soil mixes (fig. 73).

A sieve set of different mesh sizes is suggested for preparing the soil of your penjing. The large mesh removes the biggest particles, and the small mesh is used to remove the dust afterwards. A soil mix of such medium thickness will allow quick soaking and draining of excess water, while being porous enough for plenty of oxygen to diffuse into the soil to the roots and allowing toxic gases to diffuse outward.

2. Tools

The tools needed to create and maintain literati penjing specimens are the same as those for other types of penjing. They consist of the following:

(Re)potting Tools (fig. 74)
Soil sieve set with different mesh sizes, allowing you to create uniformity by removing large particles in soil.
Root hook, used to remove old soil on the roots during repotting.
Plastic meshes, for covering the drainage holes of penjing containers.
Penjing brush, used to clean the outside of pots or worktables.
Soil scoop set, used to place soil exactly where you need it.
Bamboo rod, used to tamp soil into the pot and around roots. It can also be used to remove old roots or to untangle them.

Shaping Tools (fig. 75)
Standard penjing shears, commonly used to prune away medium-sized or smaller branches.
Concave branch cutter, the single most important tool for pruning penjing. It is available in three sizes: small, medium, and large. The blades are either broad (to remove large branches) or narrow (to cut small foliage or new growth at internodes).
Long-handled bud shears, for the finest details and precision cuts. They are available in two sizes: small and large.
Garden shears, used for general purposes. They are mainly for pruning large branches or roots.
Wire cutter, used for cutting penjing wire. It is available in various shapes.
Wire pliers, used to coil wire around the limbs or to remove it.
Knob cutter, to remove trunk knobs and roots.
Metal wires, which allow you to have better control of trunks and branches, shaping them into the desired structure. While aluminum wire is used, annealed copper wire is better as it retains its holding power once applied to the tree. Wires of various sizes are needed for different branches.
Clamp benders, to alter the shape of branches.
Levers, to bend thicker twigs.
Garden saw, to cut large branches or roots that are too big for branch cutters.
Set of woodworking chisels, for creating *sheli*.
Carpenter's mallet, for use with the chisels.
Gravers, to remove bark to create *sheli*. They come with different cutting edges (hooked, curved or round) and in various sizes.
Power graver, for carving *sheli*.
Hook knife with in-shave, to remove bark when creating *sheli*.
Grafting knife, for grafting and budding.
Turntable, which is handy for getting all the way around the penjing when training and trimming. It can be placed on a table or stand.

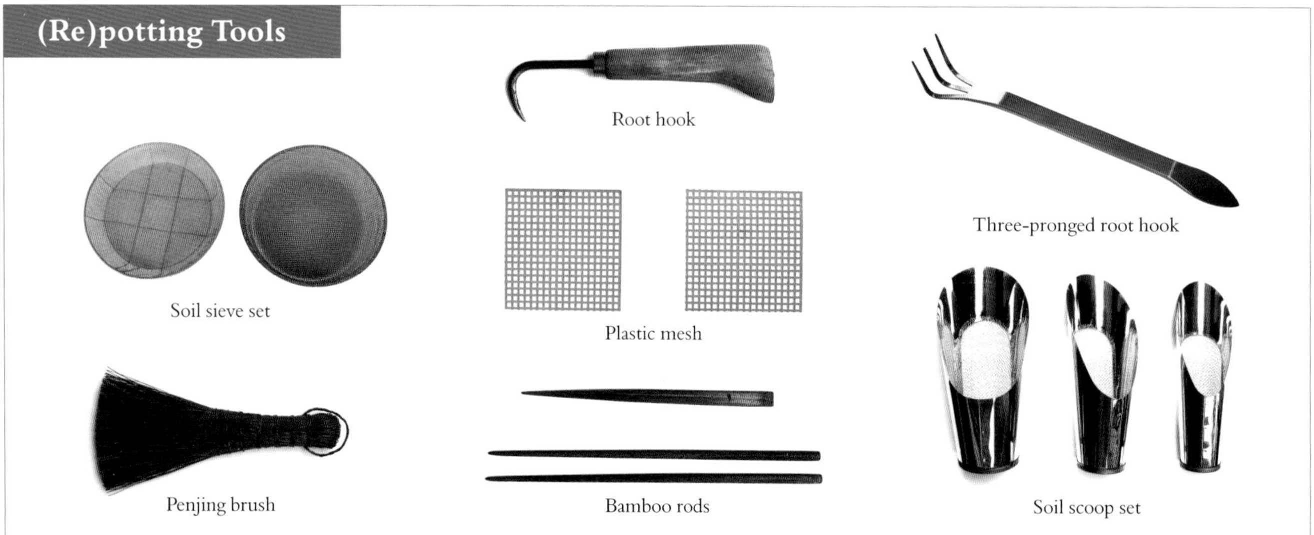

Fig. 74 (Re)potting tools

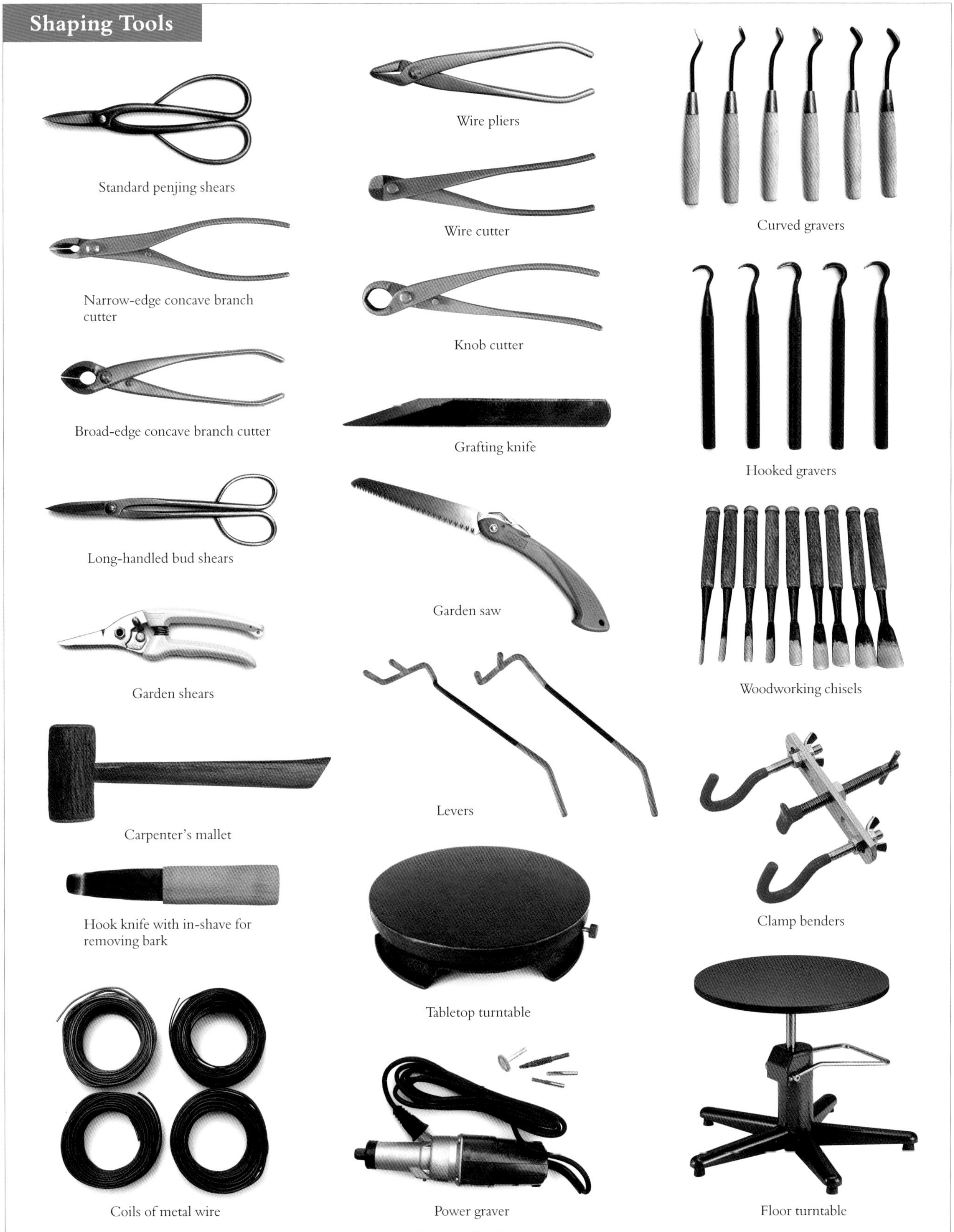

Fig. 75 Shaping tools

Maintenace Tools (fig. 76)
Watering can, with either a long or regular neck for watering and fertilizing.
Mist sprayer, for dispensing chemical solutions for pest control and disease treatment. It is also used to spray water on leaves. Usually available in two sizes.
Small brush, for brushing insects off branches.
Copper brush, to spruce up tree bark such as that of junipers.
Tweezers, for bud pinching or catching insects.

3. Basic Techniques

The starting point for creating a literati penjing is the selection of a source tree. This is followed by a tentative plan, with consideration given to attributes of the chosen tree species. With this plan in mind, the tree is wired, pruned and shaped to create an aesthetically pleasing composition. For conifers such as pines and junipers, the latter in particular, *sheli* (described in detail later in this chapter) is often used as a styling device.

The tree should not be repotted in a display pot or tray until after all the major branches have grown to their desired thickness. Furthermore, the tree should settle in the original pot for about a year or two after the completion of initial styling.

The basic techniques used in cultivating literati penjing are not drastically different from those for other types of penjing. However, their styling requires extra attention to the nuanced treatment of lines, given the work's requisite simplicity and sparse foliage.

Selecting Source Trees

Trees for penjing can either be collected tree stumps or propagated saplings.

Tree stumps can be dug out and trained to grow as penjing trees. When selecting a stump, its species, age and shape, as well as its prospects for growth, should all be taken into consideration. The best choices are usually mature trees with aged-looking and slender trunks, which show a desirable line.

The ideal time to dig a tree out is when it is in the state of dormancy, before it begins to develop in the

Maintenance Tools

Fig. 76 Maintenance tools

Fig. 77 Tree stump collected from wild, kept in cultivation container for later styling

Fig. 78 Nursery stock littleleaf box sapling

early spring. When a tree is uprooted, the branch roots and fibrous roots are kept, while the taproot is often cut off in an initial root pruning. Considering its shape and future growth, when it is pruned at this time only a few branches should be kept, considerably shortened. However, more branches should be left for pines, junipers and other evergreen trees due to their lack of sprouting ability. Stumps should be transplanted as soon as possible.

It takes considerable time for a stump to grow into a tree that can be styled for penjing. During the process the stump can be kept in a cultivation container (fig. 77) or simply in the garden, with porous and nutrient-rich soil that has good drainage, and sufficient sun. It should be planted in relatively deep soil, with bud eyes above the soil surface. Moss or lichens are often used to cover higher stumps to keep the loss of moisture to a minimum. Shading and regular mist spraying are needed in the summer, while straw mats can be used to protect it from frost during the winter. It should be watered regularly, especially during periods of fast growth. When it is dry, mist spray the leaves. While fertilizing is important for all stumps, newly planted ones need to be fed with frequent small dosages.

Pruning, wiring, pinching and control of pests and diseases are necessary before stumps are repotted. Trim regularly in a timely manner to remove dead and sick branches as well as branches that do not contribute to the desired shape. Wiring allows for control and manipulation of the trunk and branches before they become difficult to shape into position. Styling usually can start about a year after the stump is planted to settle.

Most penjing artists use nursery stock trees. They are propagated from seeds, cuttings, layering, grafting or plant division. Styling usually starts when they are two to three years old (fig. 78). For nursery stock trees, initial styling is preferred when their shape is still easy to alter, with attention given to finer curves, before they become too unwieldy and difficult to shape.

Fig. 79 *Elegance and Uprightness*
Species: Sargent's juniper (*Juniperus chinensis var. sargentii*)
Height: 100 cm
Age: 35 years
Designer: Zheng Zhilin
Introduction: The lean, upright trunk, and clean, drooping branches demonstrate subtle elegance, equilibrium and composure.

Pruning

Pruning is a primary tool for styling. Penjing trees are pruned to keep the desired shape by removing or cutting back branches so that they grow better, look more natural and have better structure. Pruning is especially important for deciduous species.

Well-placed limbs are critical to ideal lines and to the overall structure of a literati tree. Pruning may be daunting, particularly to a novice; even though cutting off faulty branches should be done without hesitation, an erroneous removal is beyond remedy. Observation and practice is the only path to mastery.

With literati style trees, it inevitably comes down to a process of elimination, often over the course of many years, long after initial styling is deemed complete. Sometimes removal of a questionable twig can indeed be agonizing. Perseverance and determination is indispensable.

Basic Pruning Techniques

Parallel, crossing, overlapping, symmetrical and whorled branches are often removed or cut short to keep trees in shape. Some of them have to be wired to benefit the overall structure (figs. 80 to 89).

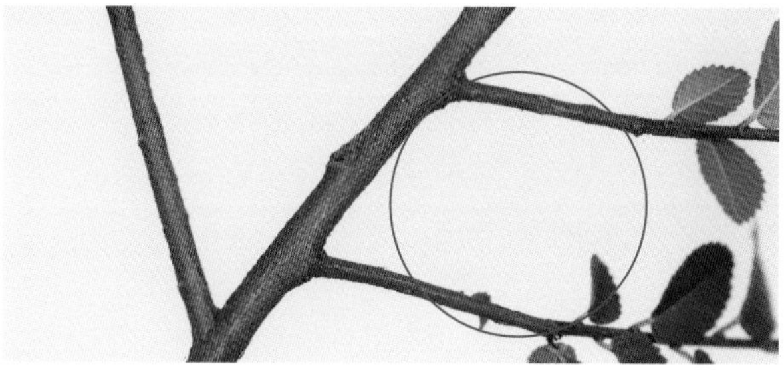

Fig. 80 Parallel branches

Fig. 81 One of the parallel branches is often removed

Fig. 82 Crossing branches

Fig. 83 One of the crossing branches is often removed

Fig. 84 Overlapping branches

Fig. 85 One of the overlapping branches is often removed

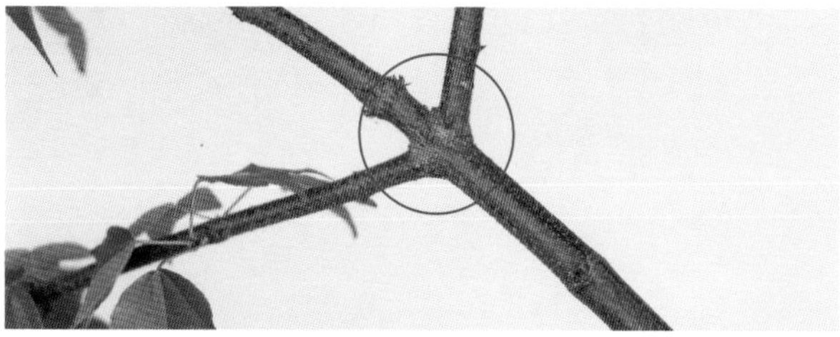

Fig. 86 Symmetrical branches

Fig. 87 One of the symmetrical branches is often cut off

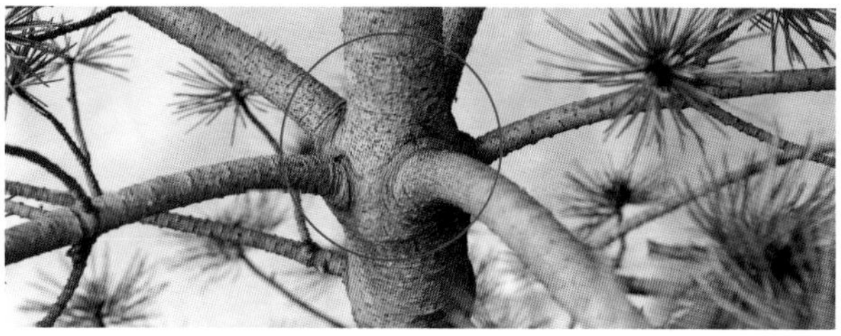

Fig. 88 Whorled branches

Fig. 89 Only one of the whorled branches is kept

Fig. 90 *Pure Delight*
Species: Pitanga (*Eugenia uniflora*)
Height: 120 cm
Age: 40 years
Designer: Wu Chengfa
Introduction: The stunted trunk, with its primary branches encouraged to grow thick, exhibits a style common to *Lingnan* penjing of southern China. The brawny trunk looks natural and unencumbered in a well-proportioned form. Hard pruning has been applied repeatedly over the years to remove unwanted branches and allow only those with the right angle to grow to the desired thickness.

Pruning Long Branch

When a long primary branch is thick enough to be pruned, cut it back to a pair of lateral secondary branches. Wait until the lateral branches are large enough to be trimmed, and cut them back following the same principle. Repeated processes like this will give you the desired structure. It is important that only one pair of secondary branches on a primary branch is kept in each pruning, and that it forms a fork with one prong longer than the other. Of course in some cases a branch may be cut back to only one secondary branch, to thin the foliage mass or avoid crossing branches (figs. 91 to 95).

Fig. 91 Branches to be pruned (primary branches)

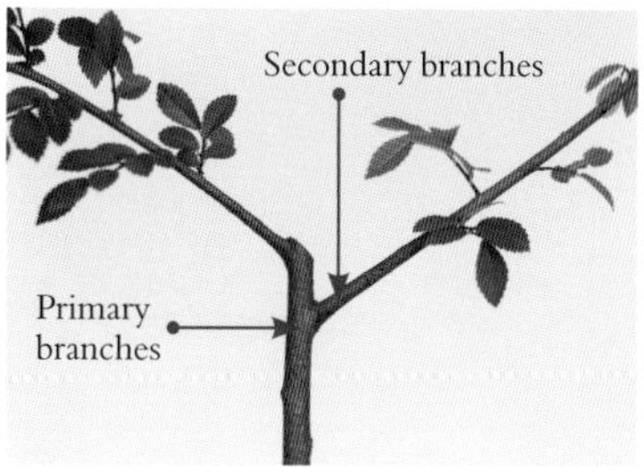

Fig. 92 Pair of secondary branches remain

Fig. 93 Well-grown secondary branches

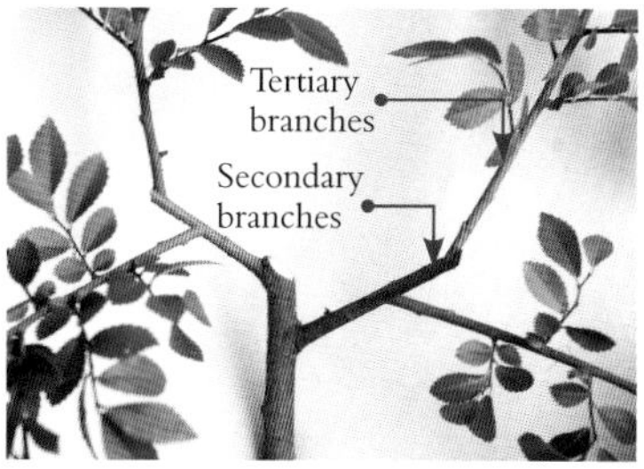

Fig. 94 Pruned for second time with pair of tertiary branches kept

Fig. 95 Pruned for third time with pair of tertiary branches kept

Initial Style Pruning

Once the front and the style of the trunk is determined, an initial pruning can be done to remove faulty branches and branches in the lower trunk, keeping about one-third of all branches, mostly toward the apex. When necessary, leave one or two minor branches on the lower trunk (fig. 96).

Decisions about further trimming of the apex should be made carefully, in keeping with the overall layout, retaining only branches that are deemed absolutely necessary in their original lengths to be wired later and to grow to the desired thickness. For pines and junipers, a few suitably placed thick branches may be kept, with their bark removed for creating driftwood-style branches.

Branches on the lower middle part of the trunk can sometimes be retained to allow thickening of the trunk, and then wired as later options for deadwood branches.

Fig. 96 Once front and orientation of trunk are determined, an initial pruning can be done.

Wiring

Wiring is another important part of styling your penjing. By coiling wires around the limbs of a tree, the designer is able to manipulate its movement into the desired position, after preliminary pruning. Such free alteration of shape is also a mode of self-expression.

This technique is used more for pines and junipers than for other species. With deciduous plants, wiring is often applied to the trunk and major branches, with smaller twigs and foliage being styled by pruning (fig. 97).

Suitable metal wire is available in aluminum or copper. The wire size selected to train a branch will vary according to the strength and pliability of the tree. Copper wire can be annealed over heat at a dull red glow, so it bends easily after cooling down. This makes it easier to apply and gives it holding power once it is applied to your tree. However, copper wiring requires a skillful designer as it does not work well with repeat coiling. Aluminum wire is generally easier to work with for beginners, and it can also be reused.

Before a tree is wired, allow the soil to dry out slightly. With less water the tree will be less distended and more pliable. For more delicate species, raffia or

Fig. 97 Wiring a Sargent's juniper

Fig. 98 Start of coil is anchored into soil.

Fig. 99 Wire around the trunk securely first and then continue upward.

Fig. 100 Wiring applied at 45° angle to direction of trunk

Fig. 101 Outside of curve, where branch bends, held with wire

Fig. 102 Neighboring branch is involved to secure control over the other branch.

Fig. 103 When sub-branches on primary branch are wired, choose every other one.

Fig. 104 Two wires coiled in a parallel manner

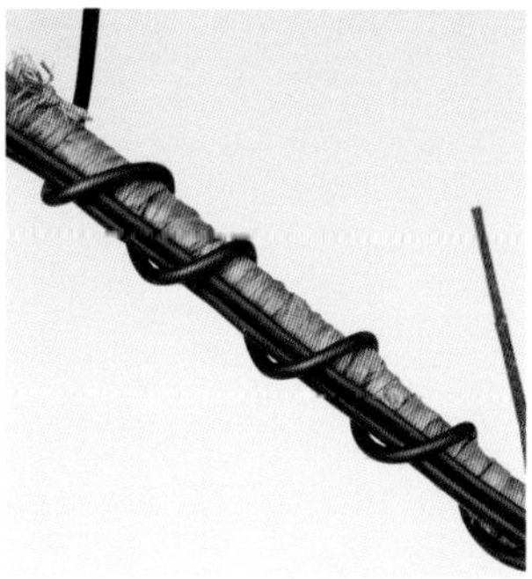
Fig. 105 Wiring a thick branch

Fig. 106 Using levers

paper strips can be wrapped around branches before wiring to protect the bark.

It is advisable to anchor the start of the coil around the trunk into the soil (fig. 98). The first turn of the wire on the trunk should be secured before you continue upward (fig. 99). Wiring should be applied first to the trunk, then the primary branches or branches at a lower level, progressing to smaller, higher branches and finally the apex. Where possible the wire should be applied at a 45-degree angle to the direction of the branch that is to be wired. As you coil the wire further down the branch, push and bend the branch with your thumb (fig. 100). Bend branches slowly and steadily so you can watch for signs of cracking and splitting. The outside of a curve, when the branch is being bent, should be held with the wire for support and protection (fig. 101).

Neighboring branches can be involved to secure positioning (fig. 102). The last turn should be reverse to the direction of the branch to secure the end of the wire.

Create movement, either from left to right or from right to left, according to the direction of your intended bend. The direction can also be changed at a fork. The wire should be cut cleanly to avoid sharp burs. A little space needs to be kept between the wire and the bark; wire that is coiled too tightly may cause damage.

When wiring choose every other sub-branch on a primary branch (fig. 103). Make sure that at least one turn around the primary branch is done to secure control of the sub-branches. The last turn should be always on the back of the internodes, with the end of the wire secured with one loop around the trunk.

When two wires have to be coiled along the same branch, do it in a parallel and neat manner because crossing wires look messy and may damage the bark (fig. 104).

Before wiring the trunk or primary branches, wrap them with raffia strips, plastic tape or cloth to protect the outer defensive layer and woody part of the trunk or branches as well as the bark. Wires can be placed on the outside of the branch where it is most likely to split before you continue coiling the wire (fig. 105). A lever may be used when bending a branch that is too thick and unwieldy, after applying padding to the points where pressure is applied, for protection. You also need to be careful not to break the branch when using a lever (fig. 106).

Fig. 107 Wiring drooping branches to form sharp angles to trunk

Fig. 108 Using thin metal wires to pull down upturning branches

Fig. 109 Removing wires using wire cutter

A branch that angles downward should be wired to maintain its sharp angle to the trunk rather than form an arc (fig. 107). To avoid breaking the primary branch at its base, it is best to wrap the fork in opposite directions with raffia strips before wiring.

The tip of a drooping branch may turn upward slightly, which can be corrected by holding it down with thin wires (fig. 108).

The length of time for wiring depends on the type of tree and its growth rate. Check often, and when a wire starts to look too tight, cut it off. Wire marks can be ugly and should be avoided by removing the wire before it has a chance to dig into the bark. Great care must be taken when removing the wire. Always use wire cutters when possible (fig. 109).

Wiring is a useful technique to alter the shape, spread and direction of the trunk and branches to create a desirable image and express your personal style. The approach to wiring should be guided by your sense of judgment based on experience, study and aesthetics. Wiring, which is critical to the success of a literati tree project, can be challenging and requires practice and utmost care (fig. 110).

Wiring inevitably causes damage of varying degrees to the bark and branches. It can be quite serious when wiring thick branches, affecting the cells that produce the bark (periderms) and woody tissues (phloem). Extra care should be taken to avoid possible desiccation. Wired plants should be kept in half shade and partial sun, with relatively high moisture, moderate warmth, good ventilation and moderate watering.

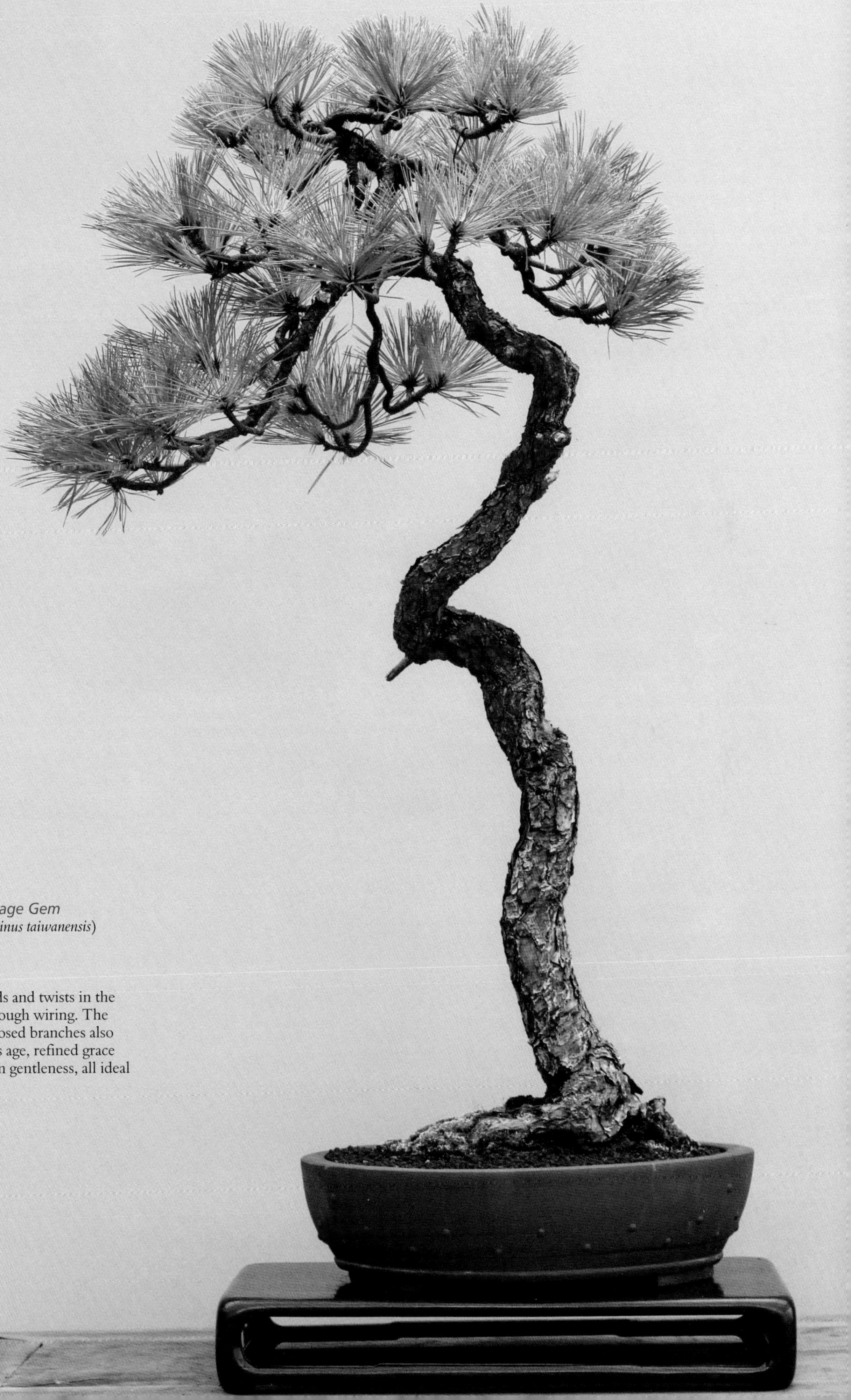

Fig. 110 *A Home Village Gem*
Species: Taiwan pine (*Pinus taiwanensis*)
Height: 92 cm
Age: 80 years
Designer: Xu Hao
Introduction: The bends and twists in the trunk were achieved through wiring. The tree, with its well-composed branches also trained by wiring, shows age, refined grace and resilient force within gentleness, all ideal attributes of a literati.

Fig. 111 Tree in the wild showing characteristics of the literati style

Sheli

An old tree, or a part of a tree, may die, with its trunk or limbs becoming bare of bark as a result of weathering by the elements or harm by pests and disease (fig. 111). *Sheli* imitates this effect. Trunks or branches, mostly of pines and junipers or hardwood deciduous species, are chiseled or stripped of bark to create the deadwood look. The contrast between deadwood and green foliage can be dramatic, demonstrating the tree's resilience and prized agedness. It gives expression to the force latent in the tree, which can be spiritually significant and appealing to the viewer.

The first rule for creating *sheli* is that it should be visible from the front together with its accompanying living part (fig. 112). The placement of the living veins should be carefully planned with thought given to their direction, twists and turns, as they affect a tree's shape as it grows.

Before you start carving, draw the desired shape of the living part on the trunk with a marker. Then proceed with removing the bark with a sharp scalpel. It is important that the edges of the veins are cut clean and smooth, which helps the tree in healing. You may want to start by keeping a broader stretch of living veins that can be trimmed in later stages. The process of debarking and carving of living veins is usually done between March and May when the wounds heal more easily.

Carving should be done by tearing off the fiber along the grain of the tree and the inner bark. The cambium cell layer and sapwood should also be removed. Such hand carving is preferred to using a power drill for its natural effect. Remove exposed white, soft tissues while keeping the dark, hard fibers (figs. 113, 114). A power cutter may make it easier to carve thicker, larger trunks or branches, before gravers are used for detailed work or strips of tissues are pulled off by hand. Use sandpaper to remove tool marks to achieve a natural look. Only proceed with carving when you are sure of your design, because debarking can never be undone. The best time to work on *sheli* is when the tree is in dormancy, and never in the summer.

When the bark of a branch is to be removed, take away the leaves first. Remove the bark with a scalpel and pliers. This is followed by carving it into natural-looking deadwood. Wire the branch immediately after debarking, if necessary, to adjust

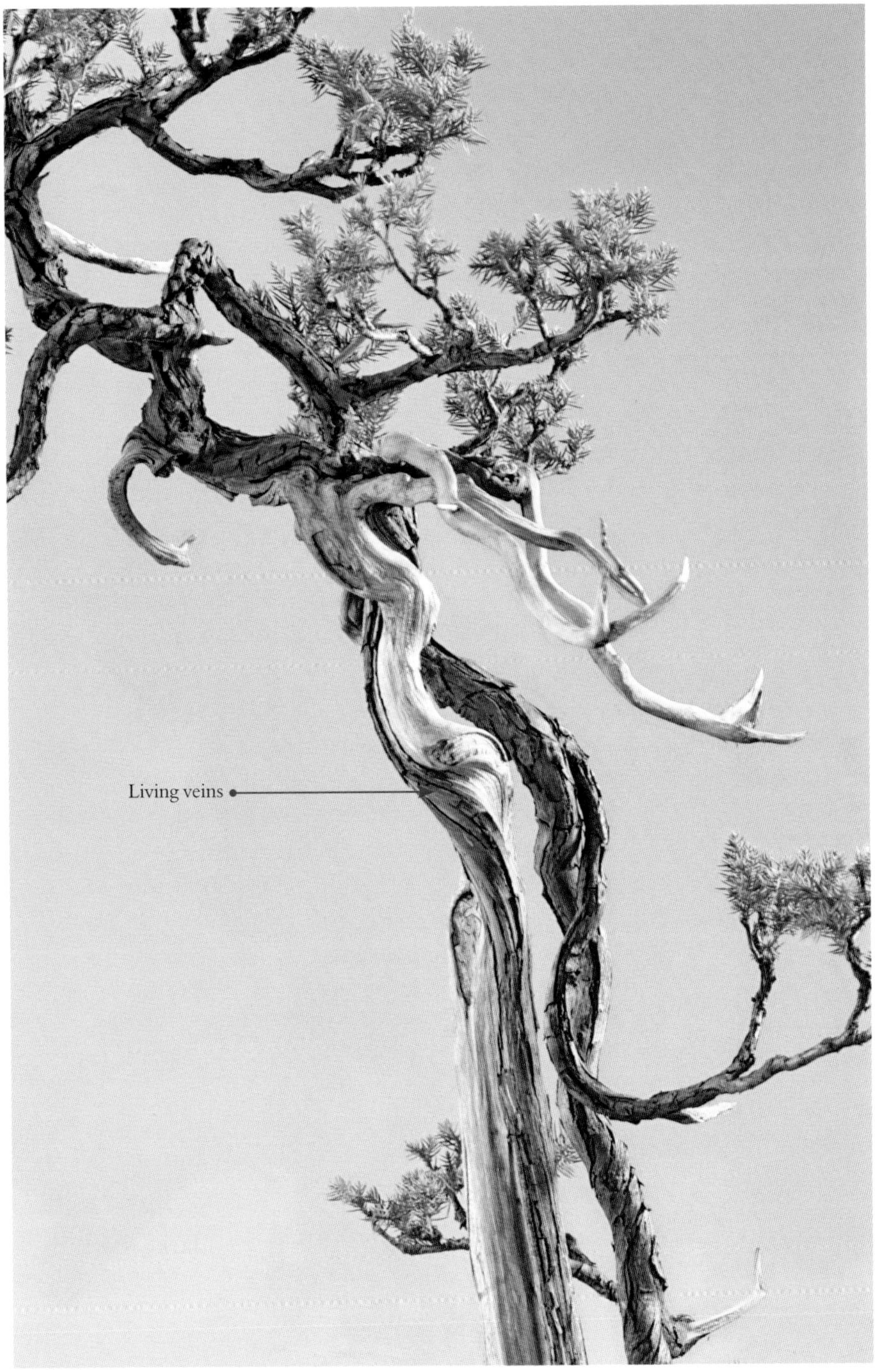

Fig. 112 *Sheli* on trunk of a penjing tree (Taiwan juniper)

Fig. 113 Using graver to carve into wood of the trunk

Fig. 114 Tearing off fiber along the grain of wood tissue

Fig. 115 Applying lime sulfur seal

its angle and line.

It is best to allow a newly repotted plant to settle before carving. Allow three to five years after a young plant is transplanted before creating *sheli*, lest the carved areas become prone to rotting.

Protect *sheli* style trees and keep them clean from pollutants, as they can easily suffer weather damage and even rot when placed outside and subjected to daily watering. Thoroughly clean the *sheli* style trees at least once a year and apply a lime sulfur seal (fig. 115). It should be applied only when exposed carved wood is completely dry and the wounds in the living veins are healed. Otherwise it may cause chemical burn.

Repotting

After a tree has settled in a cultivation container for one or two years after preliminary styling, and its trunk and limbs have reached the desired size, it can be repotted in a display pot. Shallow pots or trays are preferred for literati penjing. As the trees tend to be lean and tall with mostly upper branches and foliage, proper potting is required to keep them stable even in windy conditions.

When preparing the pot, cover the drainage hole at the bottom with plastic mesh, which stops soil from falling through and allows water to drain. Then make a wire retainer to secure the root (fig. 116). Add a layer of soil in the pot (fig. 117). After deciding on the orientation of the tree, remove some of the old soil. Prune the root mass, cutting down thick, straight and downward extending roots as well as excessive root "beard" to the appropriate size and shape for the new pot.

The tree should be held in place with the wire retainer threading through the drainage hole so that it will not be rocked by wind, which can affect root growth. The tree will thus retain its desired orientation. Place the tree in the pot, add soil and work it around the root mass with a bamboo rod so that there are no air pockets (fig. 118). Make sure that the soil is not pressed too tightly, which may lead to later compaction. Continue to add soil until the pot is filled just below the rim.

Comb out the roots before transplanting. The literati tree should be planted in medium depth, with the top of the root being near, but not above, the soil surface. Press down any roots that stick up with U-shaped wire pins (figs. 119, 120).

Once the tree is securely planted, some small grasses or shrubs can be placed to show contrast. This is followed by placing a layer of fine-grained "decorative" soil, and adding lichens and moss before the soil is thoroughly watered. It is important that the newly potted trees are placed in partial shade. The soil must be kept moist to promote growth of new roots, before they are maintained in the normal way.

After repotting a pruning is needed to enhance the planned composition. Fine-tune the shape and angle of some branches as needed before trimming, completing the styling of your literati tree (fig. 121).

A second pruning can occur in one or two years' time as the tree has settled in the new pot. Carving to create *sheli*, if required, can be done at the same time.

Given the sparse foliage of a literati tree, you should space the trimmings and allow time for its branches and leaves to recover and grow to ensure plant health.

Fig. 116 Plastic meshes cover drainage holes with wire retainers going through the holes

Fig. 117 Adding soil layer

Fig. 118 Working soil carefully around root mass with bamboo sticks to eliminate air pockets

Fig. 119 Push U-shaped wire pins into soil

Fig. 120 Hold down projecting roots with metal pins so they touch soil surface

Fig. 121 *A Literary Gathering*
Species: Sargent's juniper (*Juniperus chinensis var. sargentii*)
Height: 100 cm
Age: 35 years
Designer: Zhao Qingquan
Introduction: This multi-trunk style penjing has five trunks with the same root system. They have varied heights in a natural looking group, striking a good balance between the primary and secondary, and the converging and dispersing.

4. Design and Styling

The first step in designing a literati penjing is to select the front and orientation of the tree. This should be followed by further considerations about proportion and movement, as well as balance of denseness and sparseness, convergence and spread, boldness and subtlety, and firmness and gentleness, before arriving at an overall layout and composition.

Selecting the Front

Deciding on the front, which is usually the best view of a tree, is an important first step.

As a rule, the trunk should not bend in the direction of the viewer. The exposed roots and primary branches should spread out to the sides rather than to the front or back. The front should neither be bare nor have overly long branches. The primary branches should not have parallel or symmetrical sub-branches, and they should progress in different layers. If the trunk has a visible curve, the first primary branch should grow at the outside of a curve. The apex may tilt forward but not backward. A *sheli* style tree should have both the exposed deadwood and living veins visible in the front.

Designers often find themselves in a dilemma when selecting the best of view of a tree. For example in one position the exposed roots may look great but the trunk is not pleasing, or vice versa. Under such circumstances a decision is always a matter of prioritizing, with options to correct drawbacks later.

Facing page
Fig. 122 *Upright Vigor*
Species: Taiwan pine (*Pinus taiwanensis*)
Height: 120 cm
Age: 80 years
Designer: Zheng Zhilin
Introduction: This literati penjing of the formal upright style exhibits a simple but well-balanced structure. Its lofty form of proud loneliness is emblematic of literati aspirations.

Orientation of Trunk

Once you have decided on the front of a tree, adjust its orientation if necessary, rotating it slightly to achieve an ideal angle. A proper angle is always important, and a small change to the orientation of a tree sometimes makes a huge difference, resulting in a surprisingly good result.

Basic Styles

Literati penjing are valued as a freer, more flexible medium of expression that defies prescribed forms. Yet the basic trunk styles still apply:

Formal upright (fig. 122). This style is characterized by a straight, upright trunk, with mostly upper branches or some drooping limbs, evocative of solitude and aloofness.

Slanting (fig. 123). The slanting trunk, with visible curves, emerges from the soil at an angle. Its branches and foliage converge toward the top, with an occasional drooping branch extending in a dramatic manner while maintaining the overall balance.

Cascade (see fig. 44 on page 39). With the trunk extending beyond the tray but not turning downward, a cascade-style specimen can have sparse foliage, like a tree stretching out over the water's edge.

Cliff-hanging (fig. 124). The trunk extends well beneath the lip of pot, while spare branches progress upward, like an old pine clinging to a precipice. A penjing of this style has an air of boldness and resilience in a dangerous situation.

Curved-trunk (fig. 125). In this style the trunk, with sparse foliage converging toward the top, progresses like a twisting dragon, with an occasional drooping branch or clearly defined layers of limbs spreading in all directions.

Twin-trunk (fig. 126). This style features a tree with two trunks, with one trunk being taller and primary/dominant. There are variations to layout and orientation: for example, both may be formal upright, or one straight and the other slanting.

Multi-trunk (fig. 121 on page 76). A tree of multiple trunks, with varied heights, is displayed in a natural looking design.

Forest group (see fig. 12 on page 15). This style features several literati trees planted together, each tree with a unique character while coherent as a group. Three to five trees are preferred for a literati work.

Fig. 123 *In a Deserted Valley*
Species: Taiwan pine (*Pinus taiwanensis*)
Height: 88 cm
Age: 75 years
Designer: Xu Hao
Introduction: This literati penjing is of the slanting style, with a slightly curved and twisting trunk, foliage toward the apex, and its first branch almost perpendicular to the ground. It evokes the image of an old pine jutting out high over a mountain trail.

Fig. 124 *Acquiescence*
Species: Hedge sageretia (*Sageretia theezans*)
Height: 80 cm
Age: 40 years
Designer: Han Xuenian
Introduction: A literati penjing of the cliff-hanging style, its trunk reaches upward and stretches down after a sharp bend, as if a dragon was prancing into the waves. The tip of the trunk extends well below the rim, which also makes one think of an old tree clinging to a treacherous precipice. This stark, simple composition exudes force and dramatic movement.

Fig. 125 *To Invite the Moon*
Species: Sargent's juniper (*Juniperus chinensis var. sargentii*)
Height: 85 cm
Age: 30 years
Designer: Zhao Qingquan
Introduction: A literati penjing with a curvy trunk and drooping upper branches, this work exhibits a posture of welcome.

Fig. 126 *Double Elegance*
Species: Taiwan juniper (*Juniperus formosana*)
Height: 130 cm
Age: 35 years
Designer: Zheng Zhilin
Introduction: This penjing has twin trunks, one being taller and primary, yet all its branches and foliage converge toward the top, showing a uniquely lean yet vigorous form.

Fig. 127 Tree in the wild showing characteristics of the literati style

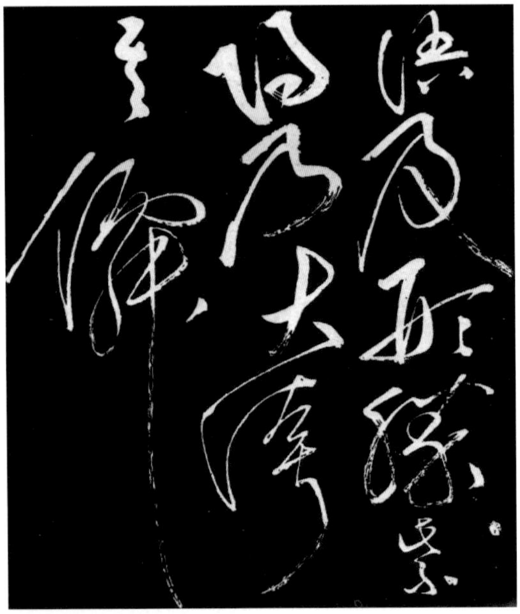

Fig. 128 Detail, *Foreword to Li Qinglian*, running style calligraphy by Zhang Xu (675–c. 750), Tang Dynasty

Fig. 129 Detail, *Entrusting a Letter to a Crane* by Shao Mi, Ming Dynasty, Palace Museum, Beijing

Creating a fine literati penjing requires keen observation of trees in nature, especially those that show aloofness and solitary grace, which are qualities to be captured in your design (fig. 127).

Literati penjing feature distinctive lines that give expression to the artist's personality and sentiments. The force and movement conveyed by such lines is akin to that in running style Chinese calligraphy, whether it is dramatic with sweeping turns and twists, or flowing with elegant curves. Viewing calligraphy masterworks can also provide inspiration for literati tree design (fig. 128).

Artistic creativity, with inspirations drawn from Chinese traditional landscape paintings (of the Song and Yuan eras in particular), may also play a role in your design. You may find the images of trees in many of those paintings worth emulating (figs. 129 to 132).

Fig. 130 Detail, *Autumn Colors on the Que and Hua Mountains* by Zhao Mengfu, Yuan Dynasty, collection of Palace Museum, Taipei

Fig. 131 *Seeking the Dao in the Mountains* by Dai Jin (1388–1462), Ming Dynasty, collection of Palace Museum, Beijing

Fig. 132 *The Distant Cold Flow and Pines* by Ni Yunlin, Yuan Dynasty, Palace Museum, Beijing

创作

CHAPTER FOUR
Projects

The design of a literati penjing starts with conceptualization, taking into consideration the basic attributes of the source tree. You need to imagine how it will look eventually and work toward that goal over time.

In working on literati style penjing, special attention should be given to achieving the desired "line" through training and pruning, which cannot be overemphasized. The goal is to not only create the ideal form but also imbue it with a particular character. This can only be done over time, usually years.

Modifications to your original plan for the tree may be necessary upon observation of its growth, which in itself may inspire new and better ideas. Resolute heavy pruning after careful reassessment is sometimes required to achieve the planned shape, though such removal can be agonizing. Indeed the challenge of creating a literati style penjing lies in perseverance and determination.

One's approach to each tree in this style may vary, as individual character is another most prized attribute. In this chapter, I will share the thought process behind some of my past projects, which I hope will serve as a practical guide and provide useful inspiration.

Fig. 133 *Rustling of Wind in Pines*
Species: Five needle pine (*Pinus parviflora*)
Type of rock: *Ying* rock
Length of container: 100 cm
Age: 30 years (main tree)
Designer: Zhao Qingquan
Introduction: This is a water-and-land penjing representing the features of pine trees growing at the edge of water. It exhibits a clear sense of dominance and subordination, emptiness and substance, and straightness and curviness. The old man (miniature) is sitting under the trees, as if enjoying the sound of the wind in the trees or of the waves from the sea.

入云

1. *Rising into Clouds*

Species: **Sargent's juniper (*Juniperus chinensis var. sargentii*)**
Height: **132 cm**
Age: **30 years**

The literati style tree most often takes the single-trunk form, with a slender and rugged trunk in either formal upright or slanting style. Occasionally a cascade or overlooking-water style may also be seen. But all have branches that concentrate toward the trees' apex.

With two- or multi-trunk variations, each trunk still should demonstrate the basic characteristics, being distinctive on its own while together forming a coherent whole.

Rising into Clouds is a three-trunk composition. The plant is a nursery stock juniper propagated in the mid-1980s. After deciding on the front of the tree, the initial thinking was to use triple upright trunks, with two on the left being formal, rising dramatically straight upward, and one on the right slightly bent and slanting. Most of the branches were on the upper half of the trunk, with very few lower branches (figs. 134, 135).

Work on the tree began in 2003 after (re)potting. Initially most of the lower branches were kept and wired at a downward angle for later pruning and creation of *shenzhi* branches (driftwood style branches) (fig. 136).

It was repotted in a larger clay pot in 2005 (fig. 137) and again into a sandy clay pottery tray in 2006. This was followed by a pruning. The remaining branches were wired to stretch sideways, forming elegant flowing lines (fig. 138). Further thinning of the branches followed as the tree grew over time (fig. 139).

In early 2014, nearly half of the branches were

Fig. 134 Front of source tree

Fig. 135 Back of source tree

Fig. 136 After preliminary work in 2003

Fig. 138 Repotted in sandy clay pot in early 2006 with a prune and second complete wiring

Fig. 137 Repotted in large clay pot in 2005 to promote growth

Fig. 139 Repotted in shallow sandy clay pot in 2009 with some pruning

Fig. 140 Repotted in shallower natural pottery tray in early 2014 with nearly half the remaining branches trimmed

Fig. 141 Back of finished form in 2014

pruned (a few were identified and kept for creating *shenzhi* branches). The tree was repotted in a shallower, natural looking tray, and its form by then was more or less finalized, excepting further trimming when needed (fig. 140).

A literati style tree is not altogether different from other penjing styles. For example *Rising into Clouds* merges the styles of formal upright, slanting and triple-trunk. However, it shows the essential characteristics of a literati tree: a slender and elegant trunk, sparse and airy foliage, unpretentious character, and a vigorous line. It is emblematic of harmony, showing cohesion out of contrasts, such as those between the primary and secondary, high and low, rugged and slender, upright and slanting, straight and bent, dense and sparse, movement and stillness, converging and dispersing, rivalry and surrender (figs. 141, 142).

Work on this project enhanced my understanding of the Chinese wisdom of reconciliation. Detaching oneself from worldly trivialities and dedicating oneself to the creation of literati style trees yields profound delight.

Facing page
Fig. 142 Front of finished form in 2014

出尘

2. A Recluse

Species: **Japanese black pine (*Pinus thunbergii*)**
Height: **106 cm**
Age: **25 years**

Fig. 143 Front of source tree

Fig. 144 Back of source tree

Solitude, simplicity, freedom from affectation, and a state of *Chan* are quintessential elements in a literati style penjing. These attributes are what I had sought in creating *A Recluse*.

It was developed from a Japanese black pine collected in the wild. I carefully observed the plant before deciding about its front and back, chiefly according to the following criteria. Firstly in being viewed from the front, the trunk should not curve forward. Additionally, exposed roots and primary branches should stretch out left and right, but not so much to the front and back. Finally the primary branches should extend from the outside, rather than the hollow, of the bend in the trunk if it is curved (figs. 143, 144).

The plant has been trained since early 2004. The first step was to remove faulty branches that were symmetrical, overlapping and densely grown (fig. 145). The twigs that I felt uncertain about were kept until I could decide later. To secure proper styling, two thick, straight wires were placed vertically alongside the trunk, which was then wrapped with raffia strips to prevent

Fig. 145 First prune in 2004

Fig. 146 Trunk wrapped with raffia for bark protection

Fig. 147 After wrapping with raffia

bark damage from the wiring (figs. 146, 147). Then, sticks and turnbuckles were used to bend the lower part of the trunk (fig. 148). The upper half of the trunk was wired to achieve the desired curve, and branches were trained to spread from the outside of a curve in the trunk (fig. 149).

After training through the end of 2005, the planned form began to take shape in the grown branches and foliage (fig. 150). Two primary branches in the middle of the main trunk were removed in the following year. After rewiring it began to display characteristics of a literati style tree (fig. 151).

Fig. 148 Using sticks and turnbuckles to bend trunk

Fig. 149 Wiring upper half of tree

Fig. 150 End of 2005 with trained trunk and fuller growth of branches and leaves

Fig. 151 Two major branches in middle were removed in 2006, followed by rewiring

Fig. 152 Top was cut off in 2011 to add peculiar touch

Fig. 153 Back of finished form in 2014

In 2011 the tree crown was trimmed, which reduced the height and pushed up the relative position of the first branch. This lent a touch of solitude and elegance to the tree, to correct the lack of character. In the lower middle section, only one branch was retained as a transition between the upper and lower halves of the tree (fig. 152). The styling was largely completed by 2014, and the tree was repotted in a natural looking pottery tray (figs. 153, 154).

Throughout the process, I used techniques to encourage fuller growth, and kept eliminating unwanted branches and foliage down to the barest minimum. Not only does the lower middle section now have sparse branches, but the branches near the apex are also widely spaced, with the topmost branch eventually being removed, for an effect of absolute stoicism.

The pursuit of such minimalist aesthetics is in keeping with the tenet of "great wisdom in ultimate simplicity" espoused by the Taoist, or the Buddhist belief of seeing "the world in a petal of flower and the power of Buddha in a lone leaf." The seemingly imperfect form is in fact a more powerful statement of the spirit. It elicits an inner peace as well as a state of being at ease with the world and as unencumbered as a recluse.

Facing page
Fig. 154 Front of finished form in 2014

临壑

3. *Over the Void*

Species: **Sargent's juniper (*Juniperus chinensis var. sargentii*)**
Height: **86 cm**
Age: **30 years**

The styling of a literati penjing allows much room for creativity, given that no fixed forms must be followed, as long as the design is in keeping with the general principles of aesthetics, basic attributes of a literati style tree, and requirements of plant culture.

Over the Void was styled entirely after a preconceived form, and work started in 2003. The source tree was a nursery stock juniper with a slender trunk nearly 150 cm in height and an age of about 20 years (fig. 155). To secure proper styling, two thick straight wires were placed alongside the trunk, which was then wrapped with raffia for protection against bark damage. A clamp bender was used for training the thicker, lower part of the trunk (fig. 156).

In 2005, more work was carried out for finer adjustment to the trunk, resulting in a smoother line and more depth to the tree form (fig. 157), with rewiring of the secondary branches (fig. 158). Again a bender was used to achieve a more precise curve for the shorter and thicker branches. Soft matting was used to cushion the spots where pressure was applied, for protection against bark damage (fig. 159).

In 2007, modifications of a *shenzhi* branch and *sheli* trunk were made in order to create stark contrast between growth and withered age, lending antiquity and scarred natural beauty to the tree form (fig. 160). Then again in 2010, further pruning was done to trim the *shenzhi* branch, which had become too obtrusive, toward the upper left, leaving only a short stub for stark simplicity (fig. 161).

In early 2014, the tree shape was largely finalized after repotting in a shallow natural looking tray. Further

Fig. 155 Source tree in 2003

Fig. 156 Using clamp bender to bend trunk in 2003

Fig. 157 Fine adjustment to shape of trunk in 2005

Fig. 158 Wiring secondary branches in 2005

Fig. 159 Using clamp bender to bend trunk, cushioning at pressure points

Fig. 160 Creating *shenzhi* branch and *sheli* trunk in 2007

Fig. 161 Trimming in 2010, with obtrusive upper left *shenzhi* branch cut down to stub

Fig. 162 Back of finished form in 2014

pruning is expected as the tree continues to grow in the future, with its outstretching branches in particular to be thinned to reduce their weight, maintaining overall balance (figs. 162, 163).

Literati style trees generally have more distinct lines than other types of penjing trees. They serve the purpose of creating the desired form, and give expression to a penjing artist's feelings, taste and aspirations. The dominant line of the trunk can be idiosyncratic and lend a distinct character.

I have given much time to observing and modifying the linear shape of *Over the Void* so its line reflects such objectives. The curvy trunk progresses upward to the right and then drops abruptly before finishing off in an upturned apex pointing to the empty sky, as if "in lamentation of the great void left by the passing of all fallen heroes," to quote an obscure 18th-century Chinese poet.

Facing page
Fig. 163 Front of finished form in 2014

古风

4. *Spirit of Antiquity*

Species: **Taiwan pine (*Pinus taiwanensis*)**
Height: **85 cm**
Age: **Approx. 80 years**

Fig. 164 Front of source tree in 2008

Fig. 165 Back of source tree in 2008

Taiwan pine has been a popular species for penjing since antiquity. It is a classic favored for its flowing elegance, evocation of age, and varied natural forms, which have been hallowed in Chinese traditional paintings. Often clinging to rocky mountain cliffs, the Taiwan pine grows extremely slowly, displaying no visible change over years. Hence a seemingly young small pine can in fact have lived for centuries.

For this project, the wild source tree, of dwarf size with ancient-looking scaly bark, was acquired in 2008. It had an aged feel with some 70 to 80 years of growth behind it, and had undergone initial styling at the time of my acquisition (figs. 164, 165). Restyling required positioning the trunk slightly toward the left for movement before wire training. As there was a curve in the upper middle section at almost a 90-degree angle coming forward, sticks and turnbuckles were used to train the faulty trunk (fig. 166).

Fig. 166 Trunk made to lean to left in 2008 using sticks and turnbuckles to bend trunk

Fig. 167 Rewiring in 2009 with continued training of trunk

In 2009, rewiring was done and a clamp bender remained on the tree for continued training of the trunk (fig. 167). In 2010 it began to show characteristics of a literati style tree after repotting into a smaller pot (fig. 168). The downward, outstretching slant of the branches was later slightly adjusted and the overall shape was finalized in 2013 (fig.169).

Further and finer adjustments were applied to the branches, with a focus on creating the ideal linear form with the attributes of expansive space and natural elegance (fig. 170). The feeling of an aged tree became more pronounced by 2014 (figs. 171, 172).

Fig. 169 Desired form largely achieved in 2013

Fig. 168 Repotted into smaller pot in 2010, beginning to show character of literati tree

Fig. 170 Finer adjustments to branches in 2013, with focus on enhancing linear shape

Fig. 171 Back of finished form in 2014

After training, *Spirit of Antiquity* has a trunk inclined to an angle with outstretching branches conveying a sense of antiquity, hence its name. Its vigorous foliage offers a compelling contrast to the aged-looking trunk, adding to the composition's overall appeal.

Facing page
Fig. 172 Front of finished form in 2014

相依

5. *Affinity*

Species: **Sargent's juniper**
(Juniperus chinensis var. sargentii)
Height: **110 cm**
Age: **Approx. 30 years**

When the root systems of two trees grow in proximity, the surfaces that touch can be abraded and the roots will grow together. Such joined roots have been used in China to describe couples deeply in love. The design for *Affinity* was inspired by the metaphor.

It was developed from a nursery stock juniper acquired in 2003. Originally there were three trunks of varying heights with connected root systems lined up in ascending order, forming a staid structure that also lacked depth. Thus I decided to remove the tallest trunk, separating it from the base for use in another project, leaving the remaining twin trunks (fig. 173).

Rewiring was carried out in 2004, with adjustment to the branches and the twin trunks to create a flowing and more varied form (fig. 174). In 2005, with fuller foliage, there was more pruning and training to enhance the line as well as to balance the competition and accommodation between the two trunks (fig. 175).

In 2007, clamp benders were used for finer adjustments to the trunk, in order to soften its ruggedness (fig. 176). Repotting into a smaller and shallower tray was carried out in 2009. By then the foliage had become too dense with the lower half of the tree appearing overly laden (fig. 177). In the following year, the first branch was made into a *shenzhi* branch to lighten the weight. However, the composition was still slightly unbalanced (fig. 178).

In 2013, after the major trunk achieved its desired thickness, a heavy pruning was done, with one primary branch in the mid-section made into a *shenzhi* branch (fig. 179). At the same time, twigs and leaves near the top were trimmed and some of the branches were wire-trained (fig. 180).

Fig. 173 Initial styling in 2003

Fig. 174 Rewiring and trimming in 2004, with adjustment to trunks

Fig. 175 Harmony of the two trunks beginning to show in 2005

Fig. 176 Clamp benders used to fine tune trunks in 2007

Fig. 177 Repotted into smaller and shallower pot in 2009

Fig. 178 First branch on right was made into *shenzhi* branch in 2010

Fig. 179 Heavy pruning in 2013, with major branch in mid-section turned into *shenzhi* branch

Fig. 180 Upper branches and leaves trimmed again in 2013, with some branches wire-trained

Fig. 181 Back of finished form in 2014

By 2014 the styling was more or less complete (figs. 181, 182).

When there are twin trunks, they should work well together while each remaining distinctive, which proves a challenge in design and training. While a unique character is most valued in a literati style tree, the composition's harmony and cohesion will be sacrificed if each trunk stands out too vigorously on its own. Cohesion should not overwhelm individuality either in a fine specimen. Thus an ideal balance must be struck between individuality and harmony.

In this composition, although the two trunks differ, one being primary and the other secondary, with varying heights and angles, they are bound via joined roots. They also show harmony in their consistency in orientation and emphasis on accommodation over competition.

Facing page
Fig. 182 Front of finished form in 2014

逸趣

6. *A Touch of Elegance*

Species: **Japanese black pine (*Pinus thunbergii*)**
Height: **86 cm**
Age: **Approx. 15 years**

The literati tree is emblematic of the refined taste and elegance of the classical scholar. The pine has always been viewed by the Chinese literati as a symbol of noble character. Thus it is a favored choice as a source tree for literati style penjing.

This tree was developed from a twin-trunk nursery stock Japanese black pine acquired in 2004 (fig. 183). Styling began in the same year, with initial pruning to remove some small twigs as well as symmetrical and whorled branches in the lower middle section of the major trunk (fig. 184). The cut wounds were sealed with a growth enhancement application to prevent excessive sap-loss, which often happens with the pine, and to prevent tree damage (fig. 185). When wiring, thick metal wires were placed along the trunk before it was wrapped with raffia. This offers easy bending and maximum protection against bark damage (figs. 186, 187).

Fig. 183 Source tree in 2004

Fig. 184 First pruning in 2004

Fig. 186 Wrapping trunk with raffia in 2004

Fig. 185 Sealing the cut wound

Fig. 187 After raffia wrapping, with metal wires placed inside wrapping for trunk training

Fig. 188 Second prune and wiring in 2006, with character of literati tree beginning to show

Fig. 189 In 2007 further trimming needed for feeling of solitary elegance; postponed until trunk reached desired thickness

Fig. 190 In 2008 leaning trunk trained to straighten slightly

In 2006, the characteristics of a literati tree began to show, after further pruning, wiring and repotting into a shallower pot (fig. 188). In 2007, with the growth of new leaves, its foliage appeared too dense in the lower half of the tree. Some trimming was necessary to lend elegance and a solitary touch. However, as the trunk was yet to have the desired thickness, I decided to wait until later (fig. 189).

In 2008, sticks and turnbuckles were used for finer adjustments to the curve, slightly straightening the over-inclined major trunk (fig. 190).

In 2011, the primary branches toward the bottom of the trunk were removed, and twigs toward the top were trimmed (fig. 191). In 2013, the primary branches in the middle section of the trunk were cut off before repotting into a smaller pot (fig. 192).

Fig. 191 In 2011, major branch in lower part of right trunk removed

Fig. 192 In 2013, major branch in middle of primary trunk removed, and tree repotted into smaller pot

Fig. 193 Back of finished form in 2014

A further prune was done in 2014, with some small branches being removed before the styling was more or less complete (figs. 193, 194).

A Touch of Elegance uses the most common tree stock and easy-to-apply techniques. It was created with much ease and a minimalist approach. Yet the composition displays dramatic contrasts between the major and secondary trunks, both slender and vigorous. Emblematic of simplicity, lucidity, a serene grace, and freedom from inhibition, it lives up to its name.

Facing page
Fig. 194 Front of finished form in 2014

天姿

7. Divine Form

Species: **Sargent's juniper (*Juniperus chinensis var. sargentii*)**
Height: **65 cm**
Age: **26 years**

A penjing artist usually has an initial idea or plan before setting about designing a work. However, a tree is a living form and changes with growth. The artist responds to these changes and styles over time, unlike building a house strictly according to blueprints. You should be flexible and guided by your sense of propriety, working with the tree's natural growth not against it.

I obtained the source tree for this project in 2004. I did not have a clear plan initially, and did preliminary wiring with the intention for a large-

Fig. 195 Front of tree in 2006

Fig. 196 Back of tree in 2006

Fig. 197 Styling by pruning again in 2006

Fig. 198 Tree well-settled by 2009 with trunk gaining thickness and foliage

Fig. 199 Carving on lower trunk to create *sheli* in 2010

Fig. 200 By 2010 showing features of literati tree

Fig. 201 Back after completion of styling in 2014

sized penjing. When I began working on it again in 2006, I discovered it was more suited for a literary penjing. After deciding on the front (figs. 195, 196), I began training the trunk and wiring its branches so that they became slightly curved at a downward angle, enhancing the natural form (fig. 197).

By 2009 it had settled well, with the trunk gaining thickness and foliage (fig. 198). I carved the lower trunk to create *sheli* and give it an aged feel in the following year (fig. 199). After a pruning at the same time, it began to show characteristics of a literati tree (fig. 200).

By 2014 the styling was nearly done, and the tree displayed a desirable shape with a slightly slanting trunk and effortless natural grace (figs. 201, 202).

The work evolved without a rigid plan, incorporating new ideas as I went along and accommodating the tree's natural growth.

Facing page
Fig. 202 Front of penjing after completion of styling in 2014

清影 8. *Phantom Dancer*

Species: **Japanese black pine (*Pinus thunbergii*)**
Height: **84 cm**
Age: **Approx. 25 years**

Fig. 203 Source tree, collected in 2006, was ideal for literati penjing.

A source tree that has a slender and tall look is preferred for its potential for elegance and simplicity, essential features of a literati tree.

This young black pine was collected in 2006. The trunk was about three centimeters in diameter at its thickest, but had a height of 130 cm, ideal for a literati penjing project (fig. 203). I started by training the trunk, placing two thick copper wires

Fig. 204 Two thick copper wires placed along trunk

Fig. 205 Wrapping raffia strips

Fig. 206 Wiring with thick copper wire to train lower trunk after first wrapping with raffia strips

Fig. 207 With wiring, trunk bent into desired shape

Fig. 208 Pruning back upper branches

Fig. 209 Completion of initial styling

Fig. 210 Reselecting the front in 2007

Fig. 211 Finer adjustments to trunk

Fig. 212 By 2009 tree had grown more leaves

Fig. 213 Styling largely completed by 2010

along its length before wrapping it with raffia strips and wiring with another thick copper wire (figs. 204 to 207).

With wiring on the trunk, I then started pruning back the upper branches (fig. 208). Because of the unusual height of the trunk, I decided to bend back the top and trained the apex into the form of a drooping branch. This was followed by wiring the remaining branches, thus completing the initial styling (fig. 209).

In 2007 I had second thoughts about the front of the tree, and reversed its orientation so that its branches would appear to spread out more naturally (fig. 210). In 2008 I made finer adjustments to the trunk and branches to create interesting lines (fig. 211).

By 2009 the tree had regained its growth momentum (fig. 212). I did some trimming before further wiring in 2010. The trunk and branches began to show a desired linear structure (fig. 213).

Fig. 214 Back after completion of styling in 2014

The work on this project called to mind two well-known lines in a poem by Su Shi: "Dancing with a moonlit shadow (in heaven) / Is no match to joy on earth." I liked the imagery of a spectral dancer, hence the title of this project.

Aloofness, simplicity and ethereal beauty, often associated with literati penjing, underscore the design for *Phantom Dancer*. Its stark form allows much room for a viewer's imagination (figs. 214, 215).

Facing page
Fig. 215 Front of penjing after completion of styling in 2014

Fig. 216 Initial shape in 2006

Fig. 217 After training and carving lower branches in 2008

9. *Heavenly Ascent*

Species: **Sargent's juniper (*Juniperus chinensis var. sargentii*)**
Height: **85 cm**
Age: **Approx. 30 years**

A cultured person yearns for an unencumbered life and freedom. The design of this penjing aims to capture such sentiments.

The nursery stock juniper was obtained in 1998 and placed in a cultivation container for two years before styling in 2000. Once the tree front was determined, the formerly upright trunk was bent into a slight curve, slanting to the right. The top was bent backward to create movement. Branches were wired downward to show the natural form of an aged juniper. A few branches of desired thickness were debarked for deadwood effects before being wired like the others.

By 2006 the tree was still somewhat lacking in the qualities of a literati penjing, because of the

Fig. 218 After another pruning in 2010

Fig. 219 Repotting into shallower tray with hard pruning in 2013

overgrowth of branches (fig. 216).

In 2008, one drooping primary branch was carved to create *sheli*, and one lower branch, which was turned into *sheli* later, was bent vertically downward by wiring. I also carved the trunk to enhance its aged feel (fig. 217).

A pruning was done in 2010, with some adjustments to secondary branches, before repotting in a shallow tray. It then began to show the features of a literati tree, though it was still slightly top-heavy (fig. 218).

It was repotted into an even shallower tray in 2013 before a hard pruning. With the longest branch to the left and a primary branch on the right both removed, the tree looked leaner and more proud with a flowing grace (fig. 219).

Styling was completed in the following year, largely meeting planned objectives. The tree has an elegant form, with hints of vigor and soaring movement. It will still need time to take on an aged feel (figs. 220, 221).

Fig. 220 Back after completion of styling in 2014

Fig. 221 Front of penjing after completion of styling in 2014

沧桑

10. *Vicissitudes of Life*

Species: **Hedge sageretia (*Sageretia theezans*)**
Height: **60 cm**
Age: **Approx. 40 years**

While conifers such as pines and junipers are common species for literati penjing, because of their slow growth and stable form, some deciduous genera are also suitable. Hedge sageretia, with its mature look, exposed roots and small verdant leaves, can be a good choice. It also offers a pleasing view in winter when it is bare of foliage.

This specimen was created by restyling an earlier project, which, although aged-looking, was lacking

Fig. 222 Tree appeared dense and congested before restyling

Fig. 223 Parallel branches on upper trunk removed in 2010

Fig. 224 Two years after hard pruning

Fig. 225 Reselecting front in 2014

Fig. 226 Wiring and training after another trimming in 2014

in simple elegance due to dense upper branches and foliage. The lower part of the tree also looked clumsy (fig. 222). In 2010 upper parallel branches were removed, which was followed by an overall pruning, with all middle and lower primary branches trimmed off, keeping only one thin twig (fig. 223).

While foliage is necessary to ensure tree health, hard pruning is necessary for styling. Striking a good balance can be challenging yet crucial. Adequate intervals between prunings are important for trees to recuperate and regain vigor. This is especially true with hedge sageretia to avoid unwanted damage/loss.

Two years after the 2010 hard pruning, trimming continued on secondary branches as the tree regained growth. It then began to show literati characteristics (fig. 224).

In 2014 it was repotted in a glazed pottery container with a natural looking shape and elegant color. The front was reversed after reconsidering the exposed roots, trunk and branches (fig. 225). This was followed by some trimming and wiring before the project was largely complete (fig. 226).

The tree acquired simplicity and spaciousness after styling over four years (figs. 227, 228). The project taught me a lesson in timing and decisiveness. Resolute trimming at the right time is crucial to the creation of a specimen with a unique character and appeal. Removing tree limbs, especially major ones on an old tree, can be tough. The hard pruning applied on this project was hardly extreme when compared with my work on other projects. It demonstrates that the aphorism "less is more" holds true.

Fig. 227 Back after completion of styling in 2014

Fig. 228 Front of penjing after completion of styling in 2014

清秋

11. *Pale Shade of Autumn*

Species: **Diamond-leaf persimmon (*Diospyros rhombifolia*)**
Height: **85 cm**
Age: **Approx. 10 years**

Fruiting trees are usually not favored, given that their fruit-laden images are incongruous to literati simplicity. However diamond-leaf persimmon is an exception. It is one of the fruiting species most suitable for literati penjing. Its grey bark, thin twigs and tiny russet fruits can contribute to an overall literati feel.

The material was the root sucker of a mature diamond-leaf persimmon collected in 2006. It was planted in a small pot before styling to enhance its feeling of age (fig. 229).

The trunk was trained from 2007 to 2009, taking on an upright look while its branches were left to grow (figs. 230 to 232).

By 2010 it began to show desired lines, while its branches continued to fill out (fig. 233). Styling was largely complete by 2013 (fig. 234). It will take some years for the tree to settle, age and acquire the maturity of a literati tree.

Fig. 229 After initial styling in 2006

Fig. 230 Training trunk in 2007 and allowing branches to grow

Fig. 231 Tree form in 2008

Fig. 232 Continued adjustment to trunk with clamp benders in 2009

Fig. 233 Tree form in 2010

Fig. 234 Completion of initial styling in 2013

12. *Convergence of Green*

Species: **Sargent's juniper (*Juniperus chinensis var. sargentii*)**
Height: **115 cm**
Age: **Approx. 30 years**

Literati penjing demonstrate signature aloofness and haughty detachment, often with a single- or twin-trunk layout. However multi-trunk or forest group designs are occasionally used. With multi-trunk variations, each trunk should demonstrate the basic literati characteristics while together forming a harmonious composition.

Usually a small group is preferred, with three to five trees at most, of varied heights in a natural looking formation. I used an unusual seven-trunk

Fig. 235 Source tree acquired in 2003

Fig. 236 Source tree after two years in cultivation container

Fig. 237 Pruning in 2005 to trim faulty and unwanted branches, and create space between trunks

Fig. 238 Using cloth strips to pull and position each trunk for better spatial relationships

Fig. 239 Desired structure began to show in 2008

design for this penjing.

The nursery material at first lacked vigor, and was planted for cultivation in a large clay pot in 2003 (fig. 235). It settled well and regained full vigor two years later (fig. 236). A pruning trimmed back faulty and unwanted branches, and created space between the trunks before preliminary wiring (fig. 237). Some trunks and branches were pulled into desired positions with cloth strips to create a balance of sparseness and denseness, expansion and convergence (fig. 238).

It was repotted in 2008 after taking on elements of the desired form (fig. 239). It was transplanted into a shallow pot in 2013, which completed the initial styling (fig. 240). In early 2014 I

Fig. 240 Completing initial styling after repotting into shallow tray in 2013

Fig. 241 After pruning in early 2014 with some upturning branches pulled down

did another pruning and adjusted the angles of the branches that tilted upward, instead pulling them down with turnbuckle wiring (fig. 241). Six months later the tree demonstrated its desired form (figs. 242, 243).

It is evident that in a multi-trunk composition, any single trunk's over-vigorous character may diminish formal cohesion. Always try to strike a balance between the individual and the group as well as between contrasting elements: the primary and secondary, converging and dispersing, movement and stillness, and rivalry and acquiescence. This may be a difficult task but it is essential to the creation of a fine multi-trunk literati penjing.

Fig. 242 Back after completion of styling in 2014

Fig. 243 Front of penjing after completion of styling in 2014

陈设

CHAPTER FIVE
Display Techniques

The placement of penjing for display to viewers differs from how it is placed for care and maintenance. While the former focuses on the artistic effects of the work, the latter stresses the living habits of the plants as well as convenience for maintenance. Aesthetic rules are followed for display to allow a viewer to see all the important features of the penjing from the most advantageous position. Some consideration is also given to maintenance, such as the regular watering needed for literati style penjing in their small and shallow pots.

Displaying penjing in different places requires varied solutions, taking into consideration the environment and background of the display space; the shape, size and color of the plant; and the pot/tray and frame. The spatial relationship between the viewer and the penjing is also crucial for display.

Fig. 244 Background with Chinese style windows that allow good light for display

1. Size Classifications

There is no universally acknowledged system of classification for penjing sizes in China. Given the sparseness of a literati tree, which makes it look much leaner than other penjing of similar height, the sizes allowed for literati penjing at shows and competitions are often increased by about 30 centimeters. The classifications are as follows:

Category / Size	Height of Tree (Literati)	Height of Tree (Non-literati)
Oversize	> 150 cm	> 120 cm
Large	120–150 cm	90–120 cm
Medium	80–120 cm	50–90 cm
Small	50–80 cm	16–50 cm

Note: The height of an upright tree is the distance between its apex and its base at the soil surface, but that in a cliff-hanging, cascade (or overlooking-water style) is measured by the distance from the base/soil surface to the tip of the longest outreaching branch.

2. Frames

It is said in Chinese penjing tradition that "the frame comes only after the tree or landscape and the pot." This means that the frame is a critically important element in a penjing display.

The frame, which may also be a platform or pedestal, is a work of art in itself. It is often viewed by penjing artists as a means of highlighting the beauty of the work by adding to its overall balance and ambiance. The frame for a literati penjing should also follow the rule of simplicity, barring elaborate pattern and decoration.

Frames can be used for indoor and outdoor purposes. Outdoor frames stand on the ground. They are often made of stone or wood so that they are firm and last well (fig. 245). Indoor frames can be placed on the floor or table, and they are often made of hardwood. Floor frames are usually about 80 centimeters in height (fig. 246). Tabletop frames are low in profile (fig. 248) and come in round, root-shaped or natural looking designs, or other shapes such as square, oblong, oval, scroll and Chinese crabapple-shaped. A frame is to be selected from any of these to match the pot shape, but its top needs to be larger than the pot placed on it.

Outdoor Frames

Outdoor stone frame

Outdoor wood frame

Fig. 245 Outdoor frames

Indoor Floor Frames

Indoor floor frame of medium height

Tall indoor floor frame

Fig. 246 Indoor floor frames

Fig. 247 *A Lone Drunkard*
Species: Taiwan pine (*Pinus taiwanensis*)
Spread: 95 cm
Age: 80 years
Designer: Sun Jianjun
Introduction: The slanting trunk, showing scaly and aged bark, leans perilously over the edge, like a man in blissful stupor. The twisting grey *sheli* displays marks of age and invokes a sense of latent force in momentary respite.

Indoor Table Frames

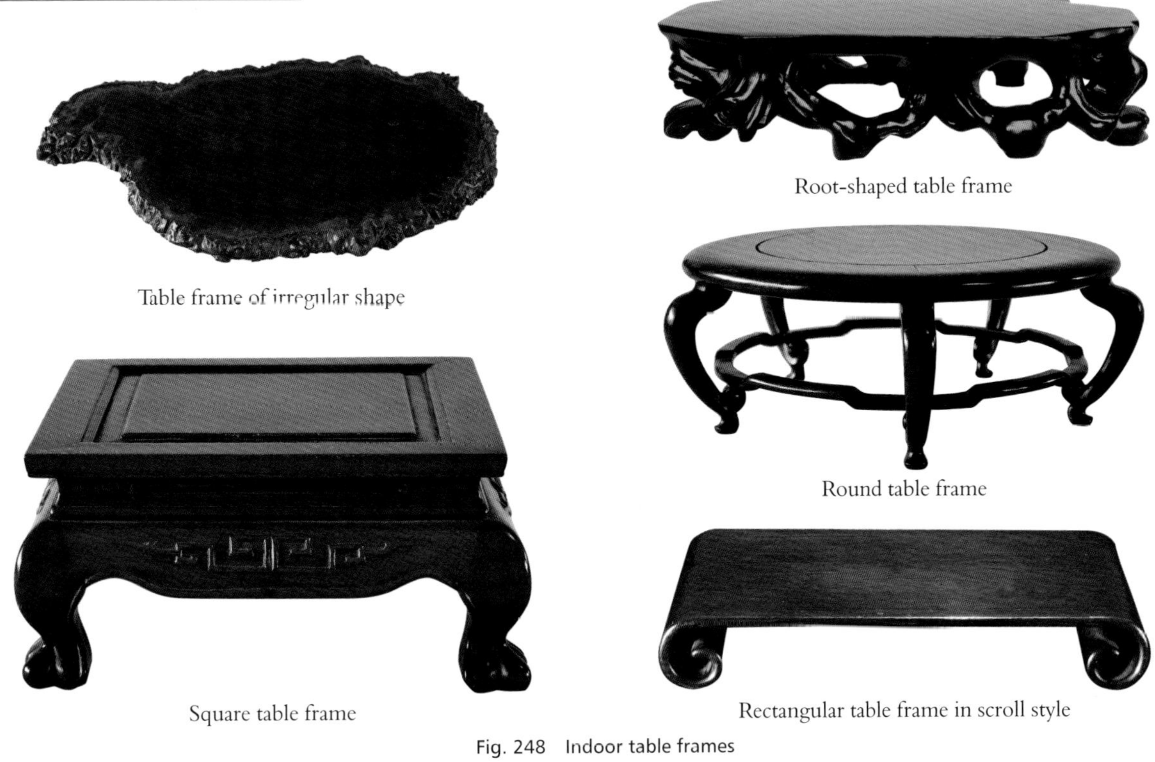

Fig. 248 Indoor table frames

3. Environment

The location for the display influences the technique for showing literati penjing: indoor displays differ from outdoor ones, and public displays differ from those in private spaces.

Many specimens are placed indoors only temporarily as they need outdoor conditions for healthy growth. Outdoor display, on the other hand, is often over an extended period of time, and growth conditions should be taken into consideration.

Indoor vs. Outdoor

As most rooms are not as sunny as an outdoor space, and the air does not circulate as well, which affects photosynthesis of plants, it is important to know how long a specific plant can survive indoors. Then one can make informed decisions on its indoor placement duration in different seasons. As a rule, penjing can stay indoors a little longer in winter as plants go into dormancy. They need to be returned to an outdoor spot in spring, particularly when new leaves start to grow. Plants on prolonged indoor display also need to be rotated outdoors to ensure good growth.

Like plants in the wild, potted plants die without sunlight, air and water. Penjing specimens need to be placed in a well-lit and airy environment. For outdoor displays, conditions such as sunlight, air and weather should be taken into consideration, with protective

Fig. 249 Background for literati style penjing, plain and quiet in color with matching landscape theme

Fig. 250 Outdoor display area, Yangzhou Penjing Museum. Background walls and structures have windows or holes to allow good ventilation and light.

measures taken in summer and winter. The placement should allow easy care and maintenance, and species with different sun/shade preferences are to be placed accordingly.

Background

The background refers to the vertical surface behind a penjing on display, such as a wall or a background painting.

Like a Chinese landscape painting with deliberate blank spaces, literati penjing demonstrate aloofness through sparse foliage. They are best presented against an elegantly plain background to highlight their artistic effects.

The background for a literati penjing should be subdued in color to match its simplicity, keeping the focus on the work itself and projecting an uncluttered poetic image. Most penjing works are designed to allow the viewer to appreciate them from the front and, therefore, should be placed against a wall, facing the viewer (fig. 249).

For outdoor display, penjing specimens can be placed in a natural setting, as part of a larger landscape and free from clutter in the background. A wall or a special structure can be used as background, but displays look best with their own dedicated backdrop. The finest often have windows or openings to allow air and light to reach the living plants (fig. 250).

Space

Penjing works need to be displayed in a space of appropriate size to enhance their aesthetic appeal.

A medium-sized or small penjing is best placed indoors on a tabletop to allow closer appreciation; a large one should be displayed in a roomy space for viewers' appreciation both in front of it and at a reasonable distance. As a rule, literati penjing require a relatively larger space to fully project the work's

Fig. 251 For display in exhibition, place literati penjing in well-lit and ventilated space, with perhaps a Chinese landscape painting as backdrop.

loftiness and ethereal beauty.

As literati penjing tend to be taller, they are best placed so that the lower trunk is at eye level. Situating them too high and causing the viewer to look up, or vice versa, will result in awkward viewing angles. However cliff-hanging specimens are an exception, and they can be placed with their pots slightly higher than eye level.

Indoor Display

Penjing specimens can be displayed indoors at home, at exhibitions, in garden pavilions or other public places.

For displays at home, small or medium-sized specimens can be presented on a tabletop frame. Some can also be displayed on floor frames. They are best placed against a plain wall that serves as background. Calligraphy or painting hung on the wall also works well as a backdrop, but the painted images or calligraphic lines should not overlap the penjing design. Simplicity and a literati style are guides for selecting appropriate background artworks. Small grass, rocks and miniatures that are consistent with the penjing theme and not too distracting can also be used.

When on display at exhibitions, while it is important to match the theme and ambience of the exhibition itself, each specimen should be a focal point and distinctive on its own. The background should be white or light gray. Chinese landscape paintings can serve as a backdrop to show the poetry of the penjing work. The halls need to be well lit, airy and have adequate space so that a specimen can be viewed from directly in front and at a reasonable distance (figs. 251, 252).

For display in a garden pavilion, care should be taken

Fig. 252 Exhibition halls require adequate space so specimens can be viewed in front and at reasonable distance.

to create harmony between the specimens and their surroundings. The preferred background should have windows that allow good light for the living plants (fig. 253).

Penjing can be placed in indoor public spaces as part of the interior decoration. Extra-large specimens are usually not preferred, as they create difficulty for regular rotation outdoors.

Penjing on indoor display are usually moved outside for watering, feeding and application of pesticides, when necessary. They should be left outdoors for a short while after such work is done before being moved back.

Fig. 253 Take care to ensure harmony between penjing and surroundings when displayed in garden pavilion.

Outdoor Display

Penjing can be displayed outdoors in a penjing garden, the front or backyard of a house, or a public place. Penjing specimens of all sizes can be displayed outdoors, subject to display space requirements.

Long-term outdoor displays share important features with displays at exhibitions, and the presentation should stress the penjing works rather than their background.

Literati penjing are best displayed in a dedicated location. In penjing gardens, a separate area should be set aside to showcase literati penjing exclusively, for best viewing effects. The placement should allow easy care and maintenance. If they are presented in the same general area, they should be placed at a distance from other types of penjing, and avoid being dwarfed by oversized specimens.

养护

CHAPTER SIX
Care and Maintenance

Penjing is a form of living art and requires an ideal environment for growth. Proper care and maintenance, including watering, fertilizing, pruning, repotting, and pest and disease control, are necessary to ensure the health of the tree, and to maintain its artistic shape and value. It is also important to note that care and maintenance practices for different tree species may vary, given their specific cultivation and display requirements.

The basic techniques required for the care of literati style trees are essentially the same as those for all penjing specimens. However since literati style trees typically have sparse foliage and shallow potting, extra care is required to ensure healthy growth and to maintain the established forms. The ideal form of a literati tree, and its appeal, could ultimately be diminished because of one twig too many or one too few. This inevitably poses a challenge in care and maintenance.

Fig. 254 Outdoor display area of Yangzhou Penjing Museum—sunny with good air circulation and moisture

Fig. 255 Literati penjing trees ideally overwinter in bright and warm indoor locations

1. Placement

Like all other penjing specimens, most literati style trees need an outdoor environment of full sun, good air circulation and appropriate level of humidity. This is especially the case during periods of growth. At these times they are best not left indoors or in the shade for days on end, which will result in poor growth, yellowing, and even loss of leaves due to lack of sun or poor air circulation.

Tree species can differ in their preference for sunlight and tolerance of shade, and this must be taken into consideration. For species such as pine, as well as flowering and fruiting trees such as pomegranate, which all prefer full sun, it is best to place them where they receive plenty of sunlight for optimal growth. Shade-loving species such as June snow or littleleaf box should be kept in partial shade, and sheltered properly in the hot summer to avoid exposure to direct sunlight.

Penjing tree species also vary in their tolerance or preference with regard to temperature. Measures may be required to allow them to thrive in different climate zones. Given their shallow rooting, direct sun exposure in summer should be avoided regardless of species to prevent scorching of leaves and branches. In the winter they should be placed in bright indoor areas or in a greenhouse to help them live through the season, with the temperature adjusted for their respective cold-tolerance levels (fig. 255). For species such as the five-needle pine, which are dormant in winter, the temperature should not be allowed to rise too high, which may cause harm and or even death.

2. Watering

Proper watering is essential to caring for penjing trees. Because the shallow potting of the literati style tree typically limits its capacity to hold enough water, the plant may die if the soil is allowed to dry out. However over-watering leads to excessive foliage growth, affecting the tree form. It also creates waterlogged soil, which reduces the ability to absorb air and causes root decay, or even the death of the tree, due to lack of oxygen.

Adequate watering is therefore most important. One guiding principle is to water only when the soil is dry, and water deeply. Normally you may tell if the soil is too dry by observing the foliage and the soil surface; if the leaves seem to be withering or the soil is changing to a lighter color, soil moisture is lacking. However it is not simple to keep soil moisture at the right level, as this depends upon a variety of factors:

- **Tree species.** Water requirements of different trees vary widely. Water tends to evaporate faster in broad-leaved softwood trees, so they require more water than those with narrower waxy leaves. The latter type needs only enough water to prevent the soil from becoming too dry. Pine and juniper, for instance, prefer soil with less moisture.
- **Season and weather.** Water requirements are affected by the season and by weather conditions. Trees tend to need watering every day or every other day on sunny days in spring and autumn. However they need watering twice a day—in the morning and evening—in the summer, with some additional watering at noon. In an arid area or during the dry season, frequent mist spraying on the ground and leaves helps to create a relatively moist environment to ensure tree health. In the winter, when trees are in a state of dormancy, the interval between watering can be increased to several days. Humidity levels can be high on overcast days, which reduces evaporation from the leaves and the soil in the pot, so less water is required. Watering is normally not needed when there is rain, and some watering is required only in case of very light rainfall.
- **Drainage of soil.** Trees growing in well-drained soil require more water at more frequent intervals than those in soil with average drainage. For literati trees, as most of them tend to be shallow-rooted with limited soil in the pot, more frequent and thorough watering is required. You need to make sure water is absorbed to avoid drying out the root zone.

Do not use a ladle to pour water, as this wastes a precious resource and leads to shallow watering. Instead use a sprayer, and place moss or lichen on the surface to avoid disturbing the soil (fig. 256). When using the sprayer, repeat mist spraying a few times at short intervals to ensure soil soaking. For trees potted in especially small and shallow trays, place the tray half submerged in a water basin for adequate soaking (fig. 257).

In areas subject to arid climes, apply mist spraying on leaves and the floor regularly to ensure adequate moisture level for plant health.

Fig. 256 Shower spraying

Fig. 257 Watering by soaking in water basin

Fig. 258 Pellet feed

Fig. 260 Diluted organic fertilizer solution applied with watering can

Fig. 259 Pellet feed placed on soil surface

3. Fertilizing

As literati penjing are typically grown in shallow pots with little soil, timely feeding is necessary to ensure adequate nutrition. However overfeeding should be avoided to prevent overgrowth and even tree damage.

Pellet feed, made from a mixture of cake food and bone meal, is suitable. Fermented to enhance nutrient levels, pellets provide balanced nutrition and are mostly odorless, resistant to insect attack, and safe and easy to use (fig. 258). Apply pellets to the soil surface and press lightly to ensure contact, allowing gradual leaching of the feed into the soil with watering and rain (fig. 259). A diluted solution of an organic fertilizer can also be applied directly to the soil surface (fig. 260).

It is important to fertilize at the right time and in the right amount. Try to familiarize yourself with various types of fertilizers and their nutritional value. The three main nutrients required are nitrogen (N), phosphate (P) and potassium (K). Nitrogen encourages leaf growth; a phosphate feed supports flowering and fruit production; and potassium enables root and stem growth. Different species need varying amounts of each element at different stages. For example foliage plants need more nitrogen while flower- and fruit-effect plants require more phosphate. The following are handy "Do's and Don'ts" for fertilizing:

- Organic fertilizers such as bean or rapeseed cakes need to be thoroughly decomposed before they are placed on the soil.
- Soluble organic fertilizers should be mixed with enough water before being applied to the soil.
- Leaves should be avoided when applying fertilizer.
- The best time for fertilizing is when the soil in the pot is drying out. Water immediately afterwards. Feeding is not suggested when it is raining, but it can be done before rain.
- A composite pellet feed is usually applied in the growing season, with only a few pellets required for each plant. Feed at one to two month intervals. When it rains for several days in a row, the pellets should be removed to avoid overfeeding.
- Newly repotted penjing should not be fertilized to avoid burning new roots.
- It is not advisable to feed your penjing when it is too hot, when the tree is in dormancy, or in the early stage of flowering and fruiting.
- Reduce the amount and concentration of fertilizer for a tree that grows too fast or is not growing well due to poor health.

4. Pruning

Careful pruning curbs unwelcome growth, maintains balance between denseness and sparseness, and enhances the artistic value of a penjing tree. Attention is even given to individual leaves and twigs. The form may be diminished simply because of one twig too many or too few.

Pruning includes apical pinching, bud pinching, and leaf and branch trimming.

Apical pinching. With this technique, new apical growth within the vigorous areas of the tree is partially or completely removed before it extends, so that vigor is distributed more evenly amongst the branches of the tree (fig. 261).

Bud pinching. Bud pinching refers to eliminating undesirable buds that emerge on a branch or fork before they become active, to allow other branches to better grow and to maintain the pleasing outline of the design. Species such as Chinese elm, hedge sageretia and Sargent's juniper need to be frequently observed for new buds that should be pinched (fig. 262). About one-half to one-third of the buds on a pine or juniper should be removed before the needles come out (fig. 263).

Leaf pruning. The display season for foliage penjing is when they grow new leaves. The new leaves are often pruned to allow young leaves to sprout several times a year to prolong the display. Leaves of deciduous trees can be pruned in early autumn before feeding to postpone defoliation.

Branch pruning. New growth brings with it unwanted branches that need to be cut back so the style of your tree is maintained. Long branches are cut short, and excess branches are trimmed (fig. 264). Common types of undesirable branches that you may cut off or redirect by wiring include dead, overlapping, parallel, symmetrical and trunk crossing branches.

Fig. 261 Apical pinching

Fig. 262 Pinching off unwanted shoots at internodes of a juniper

Fig. 263 Bud-pinching a five-needle pine, keeping 1/2 to 2/3 of budding shoots

Fig. 264 Pruning a long shoot of hedge sageretia

5. Wiring

As the branches of a literati tree may grow in unintended directions over time, adjustments by wiring may be required. A drooping branch, for instance, may turn upward; a curvy twig may grow out of shape. You may also have second thoughts about the design that call for refinement.

Wiring will enable you to maintain the original shape, or correct or enhance features of a literati tree. The basic techniques of wiring, described in Chapter Three, should not be applied to correcting upturned branches. Instead a different wiring method can be used to pull and hold a branch down.

Fig. 265 Wrapping hemp strip around node where branch joins trunk, using figure-eight knot to prevent split/damage

Fig. 266 Using plastic tubes on metal wire to protect tree bark

Using a thin wire with one end secured at a fixing on the trunk, the upturned branch can be drawn downward with the other end of the wire. Use a raffia strip to wrap around the fork in opposite directions before wiring to prevent breakage at the base of the branch (fig. 265). Protect the bark at pressure points by wiring through a plastic tube (fig. 266).

Wiring should be removed in a timely manner to prevent visible scars or damage to the bark. The length of time for wiring varies, depending on the tree type and its growth rate. Usually it should be somewhere between three to six months. Great care must be taken to protect the tree bark when removing wires.

6. Repotting

As time passes the growing roots of a penjing tree fill the space in a pot, and the soil condition may deteriorate, becoming less permeable for air, fertilizer or water. Plants that grow in penjing pots, therefore, must be repotted from time to time, to improve drainage and soil condition, and to enhance nutrition for healthy tree growth.

More often than not, it is the soil rather than the pot that is changed. Of course a larger or more visually appealing pot can be used if desired.

Fast growing species with more branches and leaves and large root systems need to be repotted more frequently, while trees that grow slower and need less fertilizer require less frequent repotting. However repotting is necessary for any penjing tree when the soil structure deteriorates and the tree is root-bound in its pot. Most plants need to be repotted every two to four years. However some penjing designed for flowers and fruits are often repotted every year.

Repotting uses the same basic technique described in Chapter Three. Gently lift the tree with its roots and soil out of the pot. Remove around one-half of the old soil, cut off dead roots, and disentangle long roots that need to be trimmed back. For well developed, densely packed root balls, it may also be necessary to trim back excess circling roots before the tree is placed in fresh soil. Trees can be positioned and secured with wire retainers at the roots. Work the soil around the root mass with bamboo rods so that there are no air pockets (fig. 267).

Repotting should be done when a tree is in dormancy, preferably in spring just as it is about to start back into growth, or in late autumn.

Fig. 267 After repotting and securing root mass, work soil with chopsticks to eliminate air pockets.

7. Pests and Diseases

Prevention and treatment for pest attacks and diseases are not much different for literati penjing than for other types. The only difference is that literati trees may be less resistant to pests and diseases due to their more confined pot space. They need regular inspection and immediate action when pests or diseases appear lest they should affect tree growth and appearance.

Agricultural chemicals cause contamination and pollute the environment, so it is advisable to use less of them. When they have to be used, low-toxin pesticides should be selected and directions strictly followed (fig. 268).

Diseases

These may attack the roots, leaves and/or branches.

- **Root diseases.** As a penjing grows over the years, bacterium- or fungus related root rots and root knots may develop. The treatment is to sterilize the soil and avoid over-watering.
- **Branch diseases.** Stem rot and canker are the commonly seen branch diseases, with symptoms that include the appearance of small areas of dead tissue on bark or woody parts, or spots on twigs. To deal with them, Bordeaux mixture can be sprayed on boughs and twigs or a lime sulfur mixture applied.
- **Leaf diseases.** Common leaf diseases include leaf spot and yellowing, and powdery mildew, causing yellow or black spots on leaves, curly dwarfs, withering leaves and premature loss of foliage. Leaves with blemishes can be removed or sprayed with Bordeaux mixture. Leaf yellowing can be treated with a direct application of 0.1–0.2% solution of ferric sulfate; and powdery mildew with lime sulfur solution.

Pests

While there is variation due to region and season, common pests include aphids, scale, and certain types of spiders and beetles.

- **Aphids.** These small soft insects of varying colors are fast breeding and attack when new leaves are budding. Dense colonies of aphids may be found along the stems or buds or on the underside of a leaf. They feed with sucking mouthparts called stylets on sap from phloem vessels in plants, causing leaves and stems to deform, which may lead to defoliation or the death of the tree. Natural predators such as ladybugs and lacewing flies, which feed on aphids, may provide adequate control. They can also be controlled by using small brushes. Mist spray pesticide when non-chemical measures are not effective.
- **Scale.** These are common parasites on penjing trees, feeding on sap drawn from stems, leaves or fruits. They vary in appearance but most have a waxy covering. Severe infestations can result in yellowing of the infected part, retarded tree growth, and even tree death. For minor infestations, scale insects can be rubbed off using a brush or bamboo stick. Removal and disposal of the infected branch or stem along with mist spraying of pesticides may be necessary for severe attacks.
- **Red spiders.** Classified as mites, they are small in size but fast breeding, most commonly seen on Sargent's juniper, particularly in hot and dry weather. Damaged areas typically appear marked with many tiny, grayish yellow spots. Following severe infestations, leaves become discolored and then fall prematurely, which may result in the death of the tree. Penjing trees need to be checked for red spiders from time to time, especially when it is hot, by placing a piece of white paper under the tree and tapping gently. When they are seen on the paper, chemical measures should be taken before damage becomes extensive.
- **Longhorn beetles (longhorns).** They often bite the bark of a trunk or the base of a primary branch and lay eggs there. The larvae feed under the bark in the living tissue of the tree for a period and then bore deep into the wood as far down as the root. Repeated attacks lead to dieback of the tree crown, yellowing of leaves and branches, and eventually the death of the tree. Adult longhorn beetles on tree trunks and branches can be manually killed in June and July in the afternoon. To kill the larvae, a chemical solution can be injected into the holes where they live, immediately blocking these holes with clay, or metal wires can be directed into the holes.

Fig. 268 Applying pesticide

8. Common Literati Tree Species

Each tree species has its own living habits and it is necessary to understand their cultivation requirements to take good care of them. While many trees are trained for penjing purposes, the species in the following table are most commonly used to create literati style trees. This information can also be used as a general reference guide to caring for trees and plants.

Species	Image	Description	Placement
Five-needle pine *Pinus parviflora*		One of the most frequently used species for creating literati style trees, it has dense and short needles, and a rugged, vigorous trunk. An evergreen tree of fine balance and elegance.	Needs full sun, good air circulation and moist soil in spring, autumn and winter. In hot summers, exposure to midday sun should be avoided to prevent foliage withering. Overwinter indoors, with temperature kept under 10°C.
Japanese black pine *Pinus thunbergii*		One of the common evergreens for literati style penjing, this pine has an upright trunk and dark green foliage with thick, hard needles or candles.	A hardy plant that tolerates cold and drought, it may be placed in full sun and in a spot with good air circulation, except in hot summers when it needs full shade against direct sunlight given its shallow potting.
Taiwan pine *Pinus taiwanensis*		It displays the classic form of a pine tree often seen in traditional Chinese paintings, with elegant, flowing lines, and an aged grace that speaks of Nature and its diversity.	Extremely light-loving, it is best grown in a spot with relatively high humidity. In hot summers, direct exposure to sun should be avoided. Tolerant of cold in the winter.
Japanese yew *Podocarpus macrophyllus*		An evergreen with dense foliage and short twigs, it displays a sense of aged grace. A small-leaf variant is more prized.	Needs warm, moist, partially shaded conditions. Move indoors when temperature drops below 0°C. On hot summer days, proper shading is necessary, and avoid exposure to full sun.
Sargent's juniper *Juniperus chinensis var. sargentii*		One of the classic literati tree species, it has dense foliage with thin needles, and a simple but elegant shape. It can be displayed all year round. Suitable for creating *sheli* for dramatic impact.	Best placed in a bright and moist spot. Partial shade is required in the hottest weeks of summer to prevent direct exposure to scorching sun. An indoor location with no further protective measures suffices for winter.

Watering	Fertilizing	Pruning	Repotting
Needs medium moisture; avoid soggy soil condition. On hot sunny days in summer, water twice daily (morning and evening). Minimal watering necessary in the winter, only when the soil has dried out.	Fertilizing is only needed in the spring and autumn, but never in high concentration or at frequent intervals. Stop feeding after October.	In March and April, pinch any new shoots to about one-third to half of their lengths before needles come out.	Repotting should be performed every three to four years, typically in the spring before budding starts. It grows well in sub-acid and well-drained soil.
Prefers drier soil; excessive water in the pot should be avoided. Water only when the soil begins to dry out, and water deeply. Reduce watering in the growing season, which will produce desired shorter needles. In hot summers, regularly spray water on leaves.	It does not require much fertilizing, and feeding is only needed during the growing season.	Pinch to remove all new needles in mid-June, leaving only two to three rows of mature needles at the tip of each twig. A second budding will come out after a month, yielding short and fine needles. Branches can be pruned when the tree is in dormancy to keep its pleasing shape.	Repot every three to four years, typically in February and March, or late autumn, with half the old soil replaced and withered or decaying roots removed. Pruning should be done at the same time for balance of the foliage and root system.
Medium moist to slightly dry soil is preferred. Reduced watering in the growing season can produce shorter, smaller needles.	Fertilize in the spring and autumn only, but never in high dosage or concentration.	Prune during the period of dormancy to reduce vigorous growth near the apex, and remove faulty branches to keep the pleasing shape.	Repot every three to four years, typically in February or March, or in late autumn. It grows well in sub-acid and well-drained soil.
Loves shade and moisture. Water to maintain soil moisture in the growing season. Regular mist spraying on the leaves in summer keeps them green and healthy.	Fertilize in the spring, stopping after mid-autumn to avoid unseasonal budding and frost damage in the winter.	Prune anytime, except in autumn, to remove overgrown twigs, diseased and/or withered branches, and to trim branches that have grown too long, maintaining desired shape.	Repot every three years, preferably in spring right before budding starts. Replace about half of the old soil; use rich, loose compost soil.
Water sufficiently but avoid waterlogging. Frequent spraying on the leaves promotes better growth and helps to maintain the lush green of the leaves.	Fertilize in the period from March to May every year, and add compost to the soil in the autumn.	Pinch the tips of new shoots in the spring and summer before new leaves develop, to keep the shape of its dense foliage near the apex. Large branches should be pruned, if needed, during the period of dormancy.	Repot every three or four years, preferably in February or March, or autumn. Replace about one-third to half of the old soil before repotting in loose, rich neutral soil.

Species	Image	Description	Placement
Taiwan juniper *Juniperus formosana*		An evergreen with short branches, dense foliage and an aged grace, it is also well suited for creating *sheli*.	Best in full sun to partial shade, with good air circulation and moisture. Grows vigorously; tolerant of heat and cold.
Procumbent juniper *Sabina procumbens*		An evergreen with curvy branches and bright green foliage, it has a graceful natural form.	Best placed in a bright, warm location with good air movement and moisture. Mildly tolerant of shade. It should be sheltered from intense sunlight in hot summers. Tolerant of cold.
Chinese elm *Ulmus parvifolia*		The elegant Chinese elm has fine twigs and scaly bark. It looks its best when it is producing new shoots in early spring.	A light-loving plant that is tolerant of partial shade, moderate cold or heat. It can be placed in a sunny, well-ventilated, warm and moist location.
Hedge sageretia *Sageretia theezans*		With aged looking, exposed roots, twining horizontal vine and tiny, bright green leaves, it offers best viewing in winter after other plants have shed their leaves.	Best placed in a bright, well-ventilated spot. It should be sheltered from direct sunlight in hot summer and from extreme cold in winter.
Littleleaf box *Buxus sinica*		One of the classic penjing trees in China, the littleleaf box is known for its beautiful silvery trunk and dense evergreen foliage.	Requires partial shade and should be sheltered from direct sunlight on hot days. Tolerant of moderate cold.
Chinese ash *Fraxinus chinensis*		With small branches and tiny leaves, Chinese ash has an aged and vigorous trunk, and tender green foliage.	It loves full sun and moisture, so place it in a well-ventilated, warm spot with natural light. Tolerant of heat and cold.

Watering	Fertilizing	Pruning	Repotting
Not tolerant of drought or soggy clay. Regular mist spraying recommended for desired environment with proper level of humidity.	Fertilize twice in both spring and autumn. A thoroughly decomposed organic fertilizer can be used as base fertilizer in autumn.	Pruning can be done in spring before new growth starts. Pinch from time to time when needed to maintain shape.	Repot every two or three years, preferably in February or March. It adapts well to almost any type of soil.
Keep the soil moist but not saturated throughout growing season. On dry days, spray water on leaves to maintain a moist environment.	Fertilize once every month in the spring and autumn.	Prune in the spring before new leaves develop. Regular pinching in the growing season helps to keep branches short and foliage dense, and to maintain the desired apex form.	Repot every two or three years, preferably in February or March. Remove about one-third to half of the old soil, and prune redundant roots before repotting in loose soil with good air permeability.
Water regularly. Water both in the morning and evening on hot days. Water less in the autumn and even less after leaves have fallen.	Feed it twice a month with organic fertilizer during growth season.	Prune in April or May, with a second prune in the autumn after leaves have fallen. To maintain shape, unwanted new shoots can be pinched from time to time.	Repot every two or three years, in early spring before budding or in late autumn. It adapts well to almost any type of soil.
Keep the soil moist and water timely on dry or hot summer days.	Feed twice a month during growth season in moderate dosage. Water moderately by spraying on leaves after fertilizing.	Train and prune during period of dormancy. Pinching off all leaves after mid-autumn encourages a budding of new leaves that will remain through winter.	Repot every two or three years, preferably in early spring before budding. It adapts well to almost any type of soil.
It prefers moisture so it is important to water in a timely manner, and keep the soil damp but not waterlogged.	Fertilize once or twice in spring and autumn. Regular feeding with a light fertilizer needed during vigorous growth in May through August.	New branches are cut back to the first one or two internodes to correct over-vigorous growth and keep the shape. Fruits need to be picked as soon as they come out.	Repot every two or three years, preferably in early spring before new growth appears, or in late autumn. Remove about half or two-thirds of old soil and trim some roots. It adapts well to almost any type of soil.
Prefers moisture and needs proper watering in growing season. Avoid waterlogging.	Prefers nutrient-rich soil; light fertilizing is needed regularly. Feed it once every two weeks in growth season.	Responds well to pruning. Pinching can be done occasionally to remove unwanted branches and cut back overgrowth.	Repot every two or three years, preferably in February or March. Remove about half of the old soil and prune old roots before repotting in loose, fertile, neutral or sub-acid soil.

Species	Image	Description	Placement
Chinese box *Murraya paniculata*		With a graceful form and vigorous branches, it produces beautiful white flowers with a wonderful sweet smell. This evergreen plant is most beautiful when fresh leaves develop in early summer.	Needs good light but not full sun, as well as good air movement, moisture and mild temperature, ideally 20–30°C. Protect from scorching sun in the summer. Overwinter in a location with temperature not below 5°C.
Chinese plum *Prunus mume*		A classic penjing tree and cultural symbol of the Chinese literati, it is well known for its shape, colors and graceful bearing.	Requires full sun and good air circulation. Moderately winter hardy.
June snow *Serissa foetida*		With a low spreading structure, small leaves, and dense and graceful branches, this evergreen produces prolific tiny, elegant white flowers in summer.	It is well suited to warm, humid and partially shaded sites, and needs to be protected from heat and cold.
Pomegranate *Punica granatum*		It produces brilliant flowers that contrast with the green leaves; branches are laden with brightly colored fruits in autumn.	It is best grown in full sun and needs a warm environment with good air circulation throughout growing months.
Diamond-leaf persimmon *Diospyros rhombifolia*		The persimmon tree has a graceful, aged form, producing brightly colored fruits that remain on the tree well into the late season. The bare, stark branches are also a sight to behold in winter.	It is best grown in a warm and moist location with full sun and good air movement. Lack of sunlight will affect fruition. Marginally winter hardy.

Watering	Fertilizing	Pruning	Repotting
Soil should be kept moist, but not saturated.	Feed it twice a month from April to September.	Periodic pruning is required to keep the fast-growing tree in shape, especially in the growing season but not in winter, to avoid loss of branches.	Repot every two or three years, preferably in April or May. While repotting, pruning can be done at the same time. Prefers loose, nutrient-rich and well- drained soil.
Keep the soil moist but not wet, and water only when the soil becomes dry. Reduce watering in May and June when shoots begin to split, and water only when slight wilting of leaves appears.	Feed it once or twice before shoots for budding develop in May, and again in early August. In autumn, fertilize two or three times.	Cut back old branches after flowering, keeping only 2–3 shoots on each branch to encourage growth of new branches for more vigorous budding. Remove unwanted branches to keep proper shape.	Repot once every year, preferably after flowering. Replace about half of the old soil with loose and nutrient-rich soil with good air permeability.
During the growing season, keep soil moist but not waterlogged. Poor draining should be corrected, especially during the dormant season.	Avoid overfeeding leading to overgrowth and loss of the desired form. Fertilize once in spring and then in autumn.	A hard pruning is required in April as well as in October. Trim when needed to remove over-vigorous branches and young rhizomes at the base of the root.	Repot once every two years, preferably in March. Remove dead roots and cut back overgrown roots before repotting in loose, rich sub-acid soil with good air permeability.
Moderately resistant to drought. Keep soil moist and avoid over-watering during flowering and fruiting to prevent over-fast flowering and early ripening.	Fertilize frequently during growing season with a phosphate fertilizer. Suspend during flowering, and do not resume until after fruiting, to minimize early ripening and fruit drop-off.	Prune in early spring. Terminal flowers will be more likely to fruit, so it is important not to cut short fruit bearing branches, while other shoots that affect the desired form can be trimmed.	Repot once every year or every two years, usually in April or May, or alternatively in September or October. Remove about half of the old soil and trim old roots before repotting in loose, rich soil with good air permeability.
Not drought tolerant. Keep the soil moist but not soggy. On dry or hot days, spray water on leaves to increase moisture.	Fertilize once every month during growing season with a balanced mix of nitrogen, phosphate and potassium, to promote full and brightly colored fruit.	Fast-growing new shoots can be pinched off at any time during the growing season to maintain desired form. All remaining fruit should be picked before pruning in early March.	Repot every two or three years, preferably in spring. Remove about half of the old soil and cut back overgrown roots before repotting in loose, well-drained, rich, neutral or sub-acid soil with good air permeability.

附录 APPENDICES

Dates of the Chinese Dynasties

Xia Dynasty（夏）	2070–1600 BC
Shang Dynasty（商）	1600–1046 BC
Zhou Dynasty（周）	1046–256 BC
Western Zhou Dynasty（西周）	1046–771 BC
Eastern Zhou Dynasty（东周）	770–256 BC
Spring and Autumn Period（春秋）	770–476 BC
Warring States Period（战国）	475–221 BC
Qin Dynasty（秦）	221–206 BC
Han Dynasty（汉）	206 BC–220 AD
Western Han Dynasty（西汉）	206 BC–25 AD
Eastern Han Dynasty（东汉）	25–220
Three Kingdoms（三国）	220–280
Wei（魏）	220–265
Shu Han（蜀）	221–263
Wu（吴）	222–280
Jin Dynasty（晋）	265–420
Western Jin Dynasty（西晋）	265–316
Eastern Jin Dynasty（东晋）	317–420
Northern and Southern Dynasties（南北朝）	420–589
Southern Dynasties（南朝）	420–589
Liang Dynasty（梁）	502–557
Northern Dynasties（北朝）	439–581
Sui Dynasty（隋）	581–618
Tang Dynasty（唐）	618–907
Five Dynasties and Ten Kingdoms（五代十国）	907–960
Five Dynasties（五代）	907–960
Ten Kingdoms（十国）	902–979
Song Dynasty（宋）	960–1279
Northern Song Dynasty（北宋）	960–1127
Southern Song Dynasty（南宋）	1127–1279
Liao Dynasty（辽）	916–1125
Jin Dynasty（金）	1115–1234
Xixia Dynasty (or Tangut)（西夏）	1038–1227
Yuan Dynasty（元）	1279–1368
Ming Dynasty（明）	1368–1644
Qing Dynasty（清）	1644–1911

Index